日本
2019

Live sport, it's a
WIN WIN

FLY BETTER

As a worldwide partner of Rugby World Cup 2019, you know we're sports lovers too. Fly with Emirates and you'll always be on the edge of your seat with ice TV Live sports and news, as well as up to 4,000 channels.

CONTENTS +

RUGBY WORLD CUP™
JAPAN日本2019

rugbyworldcup.com
#RWC2019

IN THE PACK

EDITORIAL:
Magazine Editor: Chris Brereton
Contributors: Gary Heatly, Alex Goff, Alex Broun, Brendan Nel, Francisco Deges, Iain Spragg, Hugh Godwin, Chris Brereton, Nick Moreton

With thanks to: Karen Bond, Eliott Castille, Maëlle Coulon, Diana Featherstone, Martyn Thomas, James Thorpe, Yukie Oki

SPORT MEDIA:
Managing Director: Steve Hanrahan
Senior Executive Art Editor: Rick Cooke
Executive Editor: Paul Dove
Chief Sub Editor: Nick Moreton
Lead Creative Designer: Chris Collins

COMMERCIAL:
Commercial Director: Will Beedles
Sales & Marketing Manager: Claire Brown

WORLD RUGBY:
Head of Communications: Dominic Rumbles
Content Editor: Karen Bond

PHOTOGRAPHY:
Getty Images, PA

PUBLISHED BY
Reach Sport

PRINTED BY Precision Colour Printing

DISTRIBUTED BY Intermedia

The World in Union
ワールド イン ユニオン

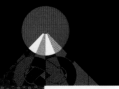

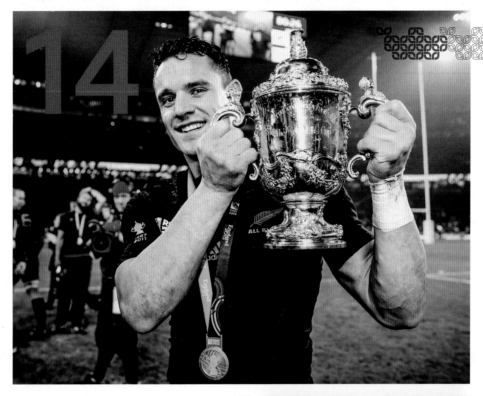

Welcome

When you think of Rugby World Cup, you think of some of sport's most iconic moments. Nelson Mandela presenting Francois Pienaar with the Webb Ellis Cup, Jonah Lomu rampaging through defences, 'that drop goal' by Jonny Wilkinson, Japan beating South Africa in Brighton in 2015 in the 'upset of the century' and Richie McCaw being the first player to captain his side to back-to-back titles in 2011 and 2015.

Each edition has a unique atmosphere, and each creates special moments and unforgettable memories for fans and players alike. That is what is magical about Rugby World Cup. Of course, England 2015 will be a tough act to follow, but on the eve of Rugby World Cup 2019 – the first tournament in Asia – I am confident that we will witness a very special and history-making tournament.

All the signs indicate that Japan 2019 will be a very competitive tournament. The November internationals and Six Nations demonstrated that there are several teams capable of lifting the Webb Ellis Cup, which makes for compelling viewing. I also hope that RWC 2019 will be remembered for being competitive across the tournament, and with Japan looking to impress on home soil and Fiji in fine form, we could see new quarter and semi-finalists, which would be superb for the global game.

World Rugby took the bold decision to award the tournament to Japan because we believed in the opportunity to grow the sport within Asia, the world's most populous and youthful continent. Tournament planning has certainly been 'legacy first' and I am delighted to say that there are more than one million new young players and countless more fans across the continent than there were four years ago – a glowing endorsement of World Rugby's Impact Beyond programme run in partnership with Asia Rugby and the Japan Rugby Football Union.

Indeed, I am confident that Japan 2019 will be the most impactful rugby event ever, transforming lives while growing the sport. It is quite remarkable to think that, through the generosity of fans purchasing tickets and our commercial family, more than £1.5 million has been pledged towards the transformational ChildFund Pass It Back programme, which will see rugby play a central role in changing the lives of more than 30,000

children from disadvantaged communities across Asia. A big thank you to everyone who has donated.

Japan will be outstanding hosts. They will put on a great show and fans will love it. It is the combination of a new Rugby World Cup destination and Japan's rich culture, heritage and famous rugby spirit of 'no-side', that has captured the imagination of fans around the world, resulting in a remarkable five million ticket applications.

Hosting responsibility will pass to France in November as they prepare to deliver our showcase tournament in a year that will mark 200 years of rugby – 200 years since William Webb Ellis picked up the ball and ran with it during a football match at Rugby School.

But until then, I hope that you enjoy Rugby World Cup 2019 wherever you are watching – in Japan or at home around the world. It promises to be one of the great tournaments, a unique and, we hope, game-changing celebration of rugby, friendship and Japan.

Enjoy the action.

Sir Bill Beaumont CBE DL

World Rugby Chairman

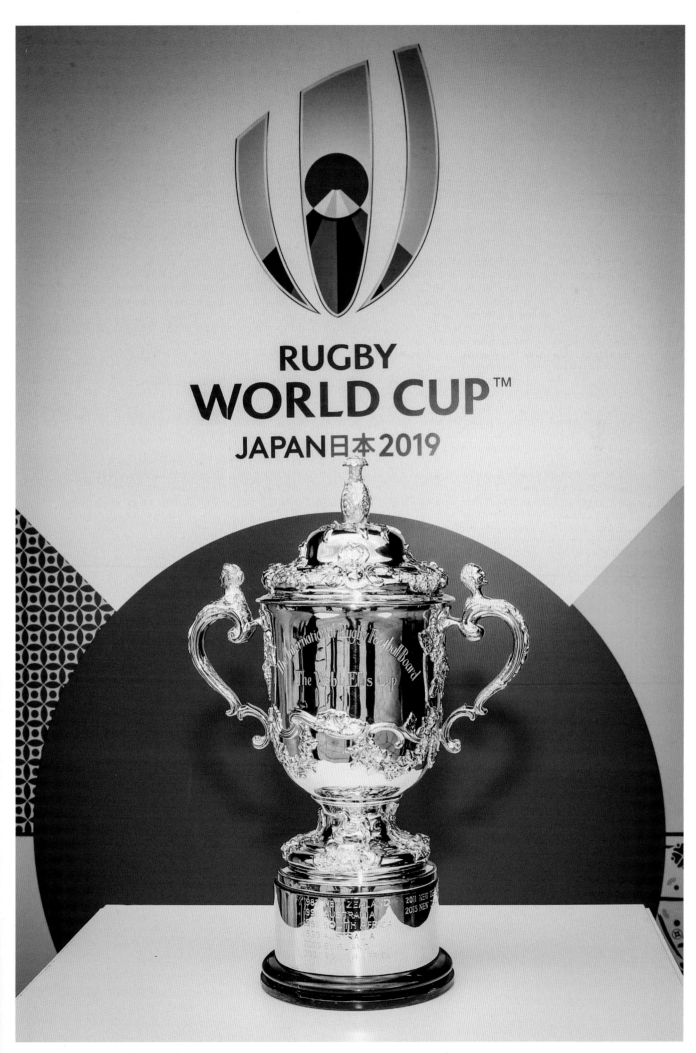

PREPARE FOR GREATNESS

The eyes of the sporting world will fall on Japan at Rugby World Cup 2019. Players, fans and all those watching around the globe are set to see the greatest tournament yet

When New Zealand's Richie McCaw lifted the Webb Ellis Cup in front of an ecstatic, jam-packed Twickenham four years ago, one question on everybody's lips was: goodness, how do we top *that*?

Rugby World Cup 2015 was a roaring success as the entire world's focus moved to England for a six-week rugby festival that showed this amazing sport in the best possible light.

It seemed as if the tournament had hit a sporting and cultural apex – a wonderful reminder of rugby's capacity to engage, entertain and unite people from across the world.

Goodness, how *do* we top that?

Well, we are about to find out.

RWC 2019 is not only going to bring Japan alive with excitement, it is going to be the biggest, boldest and best tournament in the sport's history.

Most tickets sold, most ticket applications made, fastest sold-out stadia – you can use whatever criteria you like; the proof is all there and the details show that Japan has taken RWC 2019 to its heart like never before.

World Rugby Chief Executive Brett Gosper (pictured, top right) said: "We are confident of a very special, successful and impactful Rugby World Cup that will break new ground on and off the field.

"From unprecedented ticketing demand to excellent venue and team camps and strong host city and government engagement, momentum and excitement is building rapidly, and preparations are generally ahead of schedule. We are confident that all the ingredients are in place to ensure one of the great Rugby World Cups.

"Our excitement is shared with fans. We are anticipating more than 400,000 international visitors, which will be a record for a Rugby World Cup with tickets sold from Russia in the north to Antarctica in the south. The atmosphere in venues, host cities and fanzones will be amazing."

RWC 2019 will help hugely advance rugby participation in Asia in the years to come but, on the pitch and in the here-and-now, excitement about the talent on display in Japan is almost overwhelming.

Put simply: there has never been a Rugby World Cup so saturated with great players, competitive sides and hopeful supporters.

Everywhere you look, there are stories to be told.

Can New Zealand become the first nation to win the Webb Ellis Cup on four occasions – including three on the trot?

Are South Africa now strong enough to be a true world force once again?

Will Georgia's astonishing success under Milton Haig take a further step forward in Japan?

Can Ireland fulfil their billing as one of the pre-tournament favourites?

Will Namibia claim their much sought-after first ever Rugby World Cup victory?

As the teams prepare to fly to Japan, few observers – both inside and outside New Zealand – can discount the fact that they are the heavy favourites to lift the Webb Ellis Cup.

The All Blacks may have lost the aforementioned McCaw but their strength in depth – allied to their ferocious pride and desire to improve – has seen them move on from his retirement with ease.

Arguably no sporting side in the world moves on and evolves faster or more efficiently than the All Blacks and McCaw – as well as the legendary Dan Carter – have been lauded, loved but consigned to history. For New Zealand, all that matters is now.

No team has it all their own way at a major sporting tournament, though, and the All Blacks know they are in for an almighty tussle in Pool B to quell the efforts of South Africa, Italy, Namibia and Canada as they look to cause a seismic sporting shock.

RWC 2015's beaten finalists Australia would dearly love to see their trans-Tasman cousins come unstuck – not only to make up for their Twickenham final defeat but also because it would give them a huge opportunity to join New Zealand on three Rugby World Cup victories.

Yet Australia have never been a nation that looks to others for inspiration and Michael Cheika's side arrive in Japan looking lean, focused and determined to sweep aside Pool D and concentrate on the business end of the tournament.

They will discover, though, that will be no easy task.

Wales are having an incredible 18 months, sealing the Six Nations Grand Slam in March with a stylish victory over Ireland that perhaps helped them usurp the Irish as the northern hemisphere's pre-eminent side.

Alun Wyn Jones has become a warrior for the ages, Warren Gatland as smart and as streetwise a head coach as the sport has ever seen.

Could it be Wales' turn to end their long wait for success at a tournament that has always left them crying louder than they have cheered?

At this stage, Wales have never managed to harness their true strengths and go all the way at Rugby Word Cup.

But, surely, that will end one day. Will it end soon?

Each pool at RWC 2019 holds twists, turns and interesting sub-plots.

Take Pool C for example.

It is a credit to Argentina, USA and Tonga that the pool's other two nations – England and France – are no longer considered to be cast-iron favourites to qualify for the quarter-finals.

The scale of improvement in those countries is so vast, and has been so impressive, that nobody can really foretell who will come out of Pool C intact.

England will be the favourites to do so having put their disappointing RWC 2015 campaign to bed a long time ago, thanks to the inspirational leadership of coach Eddie Jones but, as they showed on home soil four years ago, anything is possible at the highest level.

And that's what makes RWC 2019 so exciting.

England's tough task in trying to make the last eight is mirrored by the ever-mercurial and ever-entertaining French, who remain as hard to pin down as ever.

A disappointing 2019 Six Nations campaign could mean they are swept away in Japan or it could be the springboard needed to take the tournament by the scruff of the neck and amaze us all; as they have done so, so many times before at this level.

No one loses during the third half.

RUGBY WORLD CUP™ JAPAN 2019

Heineken®

WORLDWIDE PARTNER

Argentina, semi-finalists at RWC 2015, look as dramatic and as dashing as ever, combining a powerful pack with a new-look running game that can carve opponents to pieces in no time at all.

Once upon a time, a semi-final place for Los Pumas would have been a heavenly prospect but now, thanks to the huge steps they have made in recent times, it is starting to be considered the norm.

That is what Rugby World Cups can do.

They inspire teams to play above themselves, they thrill the next generation, they lay the groundwork for future glory.

Ireland are another side who cannot wait to kick off their RWC 2019 campaign.

An underwhelming 2019 Six Nations has undoubtedly dampened some of their optimism ahead of arriving in Japan but to write off Joe Schmidt's side on that tournament alone would be foolish in the extreme.

Schmidt has classy players queuing up to try and force their way into his starting XV, he has a fly-half in Johnny Sexton who can dominate a match at will plus stars such as Jacob Stockdale and Tadhg Furlong who will play for the green jersey all day long.

It is that sense of pride in the shirt that also helps make Rugby World Cup such a special event and hosts Japan encapsulate that more than most.

When Karne Hesketh crossed in the corner to earn Japan a monumental victory over South Africa at RWC 2015, the sense of excitement across the entire Brave Blossoms squad was touching to see.

That tense, last-gasp 34-32 win was a result heard around the world and has propelled Japan on in the intervening four years to ensure that now, on home soil, they represent a real threat in Pool A.

The Springboks muscled their way back into RWC 2015 after that Japan loss and finished as wildly popular semi-finalists, demonstrating the relentless forward play and impressive attacking discipline that has for so long been hallmarks of South Africa's side.

A rocky few years for South Africa means RWC 2019 has come at the perfect time for them to silence their critics and, after victories at RWC 1995 and 2007, they will be eager to return to the sport's summit this time around.

Rugby World Cups are always about far more than the 'traditional' big nations though, and it is the endeavours and efforts of some of the smaller teams on display in Japan that will provide the most life-affirming and eventful stories.

The likes of Russia, Samoa, Canada and Namibia all deserve their spots in the tournament, the same as everybody else.

NEVER GIVING UP.
IT'S WHAT MAKES
RUGBY, RUGBY.

In fact, there has never been a Rugby World Cup like it for attracting supporters from all over the planet, as described by Japan 2019 Organising Committee CEO Akira Shimazu.

"It's encouraging to see such an incredible response from international fans," he said.

"While we expected to see large numbers coming from the traditional rugby nations, I am thrilled that both the USA and the Netherlands are in the top 10 countries of international ticket purchases.

"From the very beginning, we set out to make Rugby World Cup 2019 a truly ground-breaking tournament, so to have such strong interest from fans in rugby's frontier markets like the USA and the Netherlands, as well as countries like Germany, Spain and Brazil is absolutely wonderful."

Attracting and inspiring new rugby fans across the planet is an important part of RWC 2019 and the atmosphere in the stadiums and around the matchdays will be like nothing seen before at a Rugby World Cup.

As Shimazu says, it sure is 'wonderful' – and no matter who lifts the Webb Ellis Cup at the International Stadium Yokohama on 2 November, the hand of friendship that has for so long been one of rugby's greatest strengths will again be extended to one and all.

The fans in Japan – and watching around the world – are in for an incredible time.

There will be some breathtaking rugby.

There will be friendships and memories made for life.

There will be tears.

There will be hearts broken.

There will be heroes made.

Now we just have to sit back and wait to see which side seizes the moment and claims the glory.

Indeed, their paths to Japan have arguably been more arduous – and therefore more worthy of praise. Most of all, for every minute of every match they provide ferocious competition and an unrelenting thirst for improvement and success.

Who will provide RWC 2019's 'Karne Hesketh moment'?

It is too early to tell – but it will happen.

Away from the 80 minutes of action, it is the stories and friendships made in the Fanzones, restaurants, bars, parks, and stadia across Japan that will also make this tournament so special.

Whether fans have crossed the road or an ocean to be there, supporters of all shapes and sizes and of all nationalities will come together to witness a tournament that will display rugby at its best.

rugbyworldcup.com
#RWC2019

DAN CARTER

The New Zealand great describes the injuries, heartbreaks and eventual triumph that make his Rugby World Cup story one of the very best

WORDS: Chris Brereton

"I will leave it to the judgement of others as to whether I've got a legacy or not; that's not for me to say and neither would I want to. After playing for 12 years at that level, I like to think I left the jersey in a better place than when I first started playing – but I leave that to the opinion of other people. All I want my team-mates to think was that I was somebody who gave it everything I had, every day. "

Dan Carter does a very nice line In self-depreciation and modesty.

Indeed, like seemingly everything else he's ever attempted, Carter has mastered the art.

For Carter to even question whether his impact on New Zealand rugby is up for debate perfectly encapsulates the kind of person he is.

Endlessly driven, endlessly questioning himself, endlessly looking for that extra one per cent.

It is the reason he has gone down in history as one of the game's most successful, legendary and popular players.

His Rugby World Cup story also reads like some kind of hackneyed Hollywood script. It is full of injuries, setbacks, struggles and redemptive glory.

Rocky meets Rugby.

Indeed, even at the age of 37 and with his All Blacks career inching ever further away in his rearview mirror, Carter had to spend the early part of the year denying he would be making a sensational comeback for Steve Hansen's side due to a dearth of fit All Blacks fly-halves.

Although Carter laughed off the hopes of returning for a fifth Rugby World Cup, the fact his name was even mentioned – by New Zealand's RWC 2011-winning coach Graham Henry no less – underlines once again the

regard he is held in both in his homeland and around the sporting world.

"Well you know, he's been there and done that," Henry said. "He would be number three and I think he fits comfortably in that position. And he'll add a huge amount of experience and intellectual property about the Rugby World Cup and playing international rugby."

Who could argue with those sentiments?

Knowing about Rugby World Cups was not always the case for Carter, though, an unfailingly polite, patient and funny interviewee.

Back in 2003, when he first graced the highest stage, he readily admits that the significance of playing at the tournament had not quite hit home.

"Back then they used to announce the All Blacks squad on the radio," he said. "I didn't even tune in to hear the team. I just thought there was simply no way I'd be in the squad. I just didn't think it was going to happen because it was my first year as a professional. I made my debut against Wales and then later on in that year I was playing in a World Cup; it was crazy!"

Carter's disbelief that he was about to play in Australia in 2003 was not entirely without merit.

"Back then they used to announce the squad on the radio. I didn't even tune in"

incredible in their own way. I got the chance to merge my style from those two.

"The No.10 jersey comes with a lot of responsibility straight away but at centre I could learn from those two away from those responsibilities. I could just go out there and play.

"It wasn't until we went to play in Europe in 2004 that I first really started a test match at fly-half. Everything went really well on that tour but what was on everybody's mind was the British Lions series in 2005.

"I had had a taste of the No.10 jersey and the new role and the responsibility and I felt like I wanted a lot more of that. I knew then though that I wanted to keep that jersey for as long as I could."

Carter shone in the Lions series and New Zealand, as is the custom, headed to RWC 2007 as favourites.

Yet, as sport oftens proves, pride comes before a fall.

In their quarter-final encounter with France in Cardiff, the All Blacks were 13-3 up before Les Bleus staged a momentous comeback as tries from Thierry Dusautoir and Yannick Jauzion helped them to a 20-18 win.

Carter limped off with a calf injury towards the end and the sorry sight of him leaving the field seemed to sum up the mood across his country. For New Zealand – the side and the nation – the loss was a seismic shock and the recriminations began in earnest.

To his credit, Carter does not try to absolve himself or his team-mates from blame and hints that an air of complacency had snuck into the All Blacks set-up.

"It was a tough one to take in 2007," Carter said.

After all, he had only made his Super Rugby debut for the Crusaders earlier that year and, as he points out, he only became an All Black in June 2003, making a wonderful debut against Wales where he scored a try, six conversions and a penalty in New Zealand's thunderous 55-3 win.

At Rugby World Cup 2003, Carter was a bit-part player and took part in wins against Italy, Canada and Tonga before witnessing the Wallabies' surprise victory in the semi-finals from the bench.

It was only then, upon New Zealand's exit, that the young man saw what the competition meant.

"We lost to Australia and I was quite naïve – I was just taking it all in and trying to work out how it all works," Carter explains.

"I do remember though that when we lost to Australia, a lot of the older guys were in tears. I think they realised they'd never get the chance at this level again and that showed me how important the Rugby World Cup was.

"They are the pinnacle of the sport around the world and they are what people strive for around the world.

"I happened to stumble across one in my first year as a professional but I soon learnt what it meant and what you had to do to try and be successful as a professional rugby player."

For Carter, what he had to do to become a success as an international player was bide his time and watch the masters around him.

"I played a lot of rugby in the No.10 jersey at school but in 2003 and 2004 I played most of my time for New Zealand at second five-eighths, or centre as you guys call it," Carter said.

"In those two years I had the chance to play outside Andrew Mehrtens, a player I had huge respect for and idolised in my teenage years, and also outside Carlos Spencer. Both fly-halves were completely different but

Get closer to the game with Mastercard®

Mastercard is your access pass into a world of exclusive experiences at Rugby World Cup 2019™.

Learn more at priceless.com

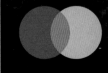

RUGBY WORLD CUP JAPAN 2019

official card

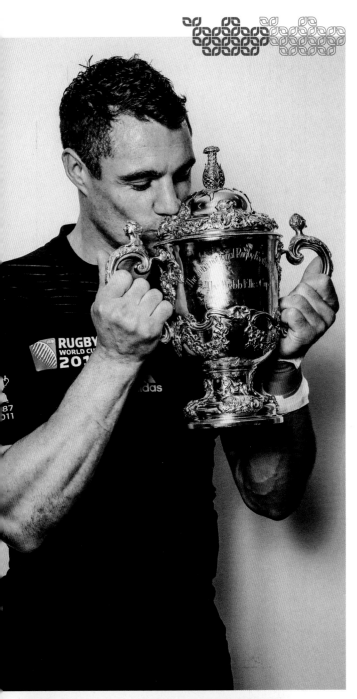

"We didn't deserve to win and we learnt so much. For me, that was the start of something exciting – everything that came after 2007 started there"

"We had been in amazing form since 2005, everything was running so smoothly and I felt I was playing the best rugby I'd ever played.

"After seeing in the end what 2003 meant, I wanted to put everything I possibly could into winning in 2007 and everything was going so smoothly.

"It was all rosey and all we had to do was turn up and we would win: as simple as that. That's kind of the mentality we went into the tournament with. It obviously all went badly wrong and it was a huge wake up call for us.

"We didn't deserve to win it and we learnt so much from that tournament. For me, that was the start of something exciting that was about to happen – everything that came after 2007 started there."

What 'started there' was the road to glory at RWC 2011.

Yet, once again, Carter's own recollection of competing at a Rugby World Cup would be tinged with personal disappointment.

By 2011, Carter was indisputably the best fly-half on the planet and the All Blacks were purring along nicely ahead of RWC 2011 in their own country.

Everything appeared set for Carter to shine, which, early on he did.

Yet after helping New Zealand cruise past France in a Pool A encounter, Carter began to prepare for a match against Canada.

All was going to plan in a training session when, all of a sudden, this New Zealand great was felled by a torn groin muscle.

Images of Carter lying on the ground, in agony, flew around the world and once again New Zealand rugby fans feared the worst.

They were right too. Team doctor Deb Robinson assessed Carter and the prognosis was crystal clear: his Rugby World Cup was over.

For the rest of of the tournament, Carter was a spectator as New Zealand withheld incredible pressure on home soil to finally inch past France 8-7 in an epic final full of breathless defence and a rearguard effort inside their own 22 that deserves to be remembered as one of the finest the game has ever seen.

Carter joined in the celebrations in his team suit but admits he struggled with how to celebrate the end of New Zealand's 24-year wait to lift the Webb Ellis Cup.

"I have mixed emotions to be honest," he said.

"I'm really proud of the team and the way they went on to win the World Cup. I felt I was in my prime; I was 29 and that is a great playing age.

"I thought that was my time. It was in New Zealand in front of my friends and family. It felt like my time to shine

and to hold the Webb Ellis Cup at the end of it.

"For that to be taken away in such traumatic fashion was a really, really hard thing to take. I've always said through my career that injuries happen for a reason because your work-rate is too much, or you're playing too much or you're not training properly, but this injury, and the severity of it, made no sense at all. I couldn't work it out and it wasn't fair. It was a really, really tough thing to cope with.

"Behind closed doors I was really struggling but when I was with the team it was about the bigger group and keeping a positive attitude around the guys, and it was about helping them. I was gutted, absolutely gutted. I was constantly asking in my head, 'Why me? Why now?'

"I had to put that to one side though and help the other fly-halves prepare to win the tournament.

"After that moment, I realised that I had to go to one more Rugby World Cup. I'd been to three and none had gone well for me on a personal level.

"I was obviously massively proud of winning in New Zealand but for me personally it hadn't gone well. I was going to give it everything to get to one more."

He sure did just that.

As RWC 2015 approached, Carter's kicking, game-management and self-belief was as good as it had ever been. The All Blacks arrived in England in great physical and mental condition and were, once again, hailed as the favourites.

"I know that my mindset going into that World Cup was great," Carter said.

"I knew nothing was going to get in the way because I'd prepared harder mentally and physically than ever before.

"Looking back on it now, I feel a bit shocked about how I was able to play. A lot of that was to do with the setbacks in 2003, 2007 and 2011 and that made the victory all the more sweeter."

New Zealand topped Pool C after victories over Argentina, Namibia, Georgia and Tonga before 17 points from Carter helped the All Blacks steamroll France in the quarter-finals.

Carter was again imperious in a breathtakingly intense semi-final against South Africa at Twickenham, that New Zealand squeezed 20-18.

That win meant that, for the first time, the best fly-half of his generation would be starting in a Rugby World Cup final. Yet Carter had been around long enough by now to understand that fairytales are precisely that. Nothing is

> "I was obviously massively proud of us winning but for me personally it hadn't gone well. I was going to give it everything to get to one more"

given, nothing is gifted, nothing is granted in elite sport.

If he wanted to be on the pitch to celebrate an All Blacks Rugby World Cup victory, he'd have to earn it over the 80 minutes, the same as everybody else.

"Just because it was my last test match meant nothing," he said. "I think there were seven of us playing our last matches. That doesn't mean anything or guarantee anything and you can't expect to go out on a high."

Carter is spot on yet anybody who witnessed his extraordinary performance against Australia will attest that, for once, the script did go to plan.

The final, a trans-Tasman derby, was intense and relentless and it could have swung either way until a huge Carter drop goal after 70 minutes punctured Australia's resurgent belief and set the All Blacks on the way to an eventual 34-17 victory.

Finally, when referee Nigel Owens blew his whistle, Carter's journey to Rugby World Cup glory was complete. Added to lifting the Webb Ellis Cup, he was also named as the Rugby World Cup 2015 Player of the Tournament, World Rugby Player of the Year for 2015 and he finished his career as the all-time leading test points scorer with 1,598. All in all then, not a bad way to go out – and he was determined to enjoy it.

"It was an incredible team effort and it was quite strange because the feeling was different to 2011," he said.

"In 2011 it was just a total and utter feeling of relief. In 2015, the weight was off our shoulders so we could enjoy it a lot more. There was a real sense of happiness. We wanted to create history and win back-to-back Rugby World Cups and there was a real sense of happiness that we had achieved what we wanted to do."

Carter will emphatically not be featuring in Japan because not only is he happily retired from international rugby, he is also currently rehabilitating after neck surgery earlier this year.

That ended any potential involvement with Racing 92, the club he played for between 2015 and 2018, but once he is fully fit, he will be back to pull the strings for Japanese club Kobelco Steelers.

That move to Japan was a huge endorsement of the country's domestic league and it leaves Carter well placed to judge how Japan has embraced RWC 2019 and what the country will offer rugby fans from across the planet.

"Japan is an amazing place," he said. "People are really, really looking forward to the tournament.

"All of a sudden we are seeing rugby becoming bigger and bigger. Japanese rugby is getting stronger and stronger and this tournament will undoubtedly help that.

"It is such a beautiful country with a really unique culture. The Japanese are perfectionists and they will have made sure that absolutely everything possible has been put in place to make it an amazing World Cup."

Carter also believes that RWC 2019 is the perfect way to grow the game in Japan and beyond. For the first time, Asia will get to see the world's best players taking part in its biggest tournament and the knock-on effects of that could be huge.

"Hosting a Rugby World Cup is the best way of getting the next generation interested in the sport," Carter said. "I remember 1987 in New Zealand and I started playing myself after the 1995 tournament in South Africa. There will be no better way of growing the sport in Japan and Asia than by hosting this Rugby World Cup. Rugby in Japan is already a huge sport but now it's going to be massive."

So who will win it? That is the biggest question on everybody's lips and Carter is happily and unashamedly biased in favour of his countrymen. Most of all, though, he is just excited to be watching it alongside those of us whose dreams of playing at a Rugby World Cup will have to remain forever unfulfilled.

"Being an All Black myself for a few years means that for the first time since the 1999 tournament, I get to watch it as a fan, the same as everyone else," he grins.

"It's been a long time but I cannot wait. A Rugby World Cup is the pinnacle of our sport. It means everything to the players and what they have been building towards for so long so it is massive.

"I would obviously love to see New Zealand do the 'three-peat' and win the tournament for the third straight time but there are so many good teams at the tournament. Wales, England, Ireland, South Africa; they all know how to prepare for this tournament and they will all be strong so it could be really open."

Carter's time is nearly up. Throughout the interview he has wanted to talk about rugby's wider values and the spirit of the sport.

For those attending RWC 2019 as players he believes they will leave Japan as better and more well-rounded sportsmen and human beings.

The spectators watching, in Japan and beyond, will also be enriched by the tournament.

"Some of my fondest memories of Rugby World Cups are playing against the smaller nations," Carter said.

"We played Portugal in 2007 and we scored over 100 points but after the match we went back out onto the pitch to do some fitness work and they were out there on the field as well.

"We found a soccer ball from somewhere, started kicking it around and then they easily beat us! We laughed and shared stories and books and gifts and that's what sport and Rugby World Cups are about; it's about making bonds and enjoying yourself.

"Rugby teaches us values about teamwork and how the team comes first, it teaches you humility, you need to remain humble and never think you're better than anybody else and it teaches you resilience and how to handle setbacks.

"Sometimes you have to go again and again and after a difficult time you have to keep trying to bounce back."

Carter certainly did that. And Rugby World Cup history is all the better for it.

RUGBY WORLD CUP™
JAPAN 日本 2019
WORLDWIDE PARTNER

THE MORE YOU LOVE SOMETHING, THE FURTHER YOU TAKE IT

SOCIETE GENERALE

THE FUTURE IS YOU

 SOCIETE GENERALE

POWER LIST

Over the next 36 pages, learn all you need to know about the greatest rugby players on earth.

From the young speedsteers looking to shine at their first Rugby World Cup to the veterans who have been there and done it plenty of times before, players of all shapes, sizes, ages and abilities will be looking to shine in Japan.

25-31
RISING STARS
- they're young, hungry and desperate to demonstrate their prowess

32-39
MAGIC MEN
- they can change a match in an instant

41-47
LEADERS OF THE PACK
- rugby's true warriors who possess both power and poise

48-53
MASTERS
- these players are worth the entrance fee alone

54-60
FAST AND FLUENT
- these stars can leave defences dizzy. Irresistible.

ADAM HASTINGS

STATS
Date of Birth: 05/10/1996
Height: 1.85m
Place of Birth: Edinburgh, Scotland
Club: Glasgow Warriors
Position: Fly-half
Test Debut: v Canada, 2018

If you play rugby in Scotland and your surname is Hastings, you know you have a lot to live up to.

Gavin Hastings is a rugby legend and is in the top 20 points-scorers of all time, while brother Scott played with distinction in the same Scotland team in the 1980s and '90s.

Gavin's son, Adam, is now making his own way in the game and the early signs are that some of his dad's talent has rubbed off on him.

Adam plays for Glasgow Warriors after coming through the academy at Bath and making a few appearances for their first team. His willingness to attack the line has caught the eye at Glasgow and he has scored 242 points in 32 career appearances for them.

The fly-half has played internationally for Scotland at U16, U18, U19 and U20 level before making his test debut against Canada in 2018. His athleticism has also been put to good use by representing Scotland Schools at the javelin.

His early endeavours at international level were impressive enough to mean he gained seven caps during his first year playing for Scotland. One of those matches saw him impress in a record 44-15 win against Argentina on tour in 2018.

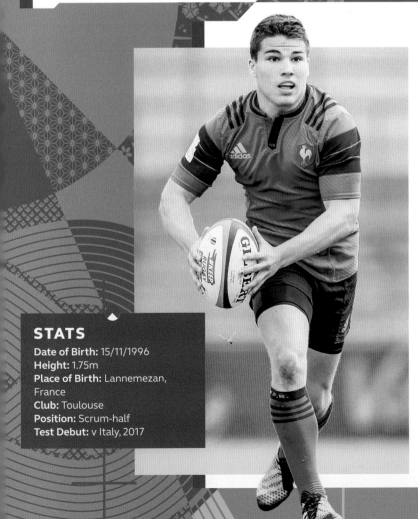

FRANCE RUGBY

ANTOINE DUPONT

STATS
Date of Birth: 15/11/1996
Height: 1.75m
Place of Birth: Lannemezan, France
Club: Toulouse
Position: Scrum-half
Test Debut: v Italy, 2017

Antoine Dupont's life was mapped out for him from an early age, having only been five years old when he first took up rugby.

His talent was spotted at every stage of his development and as he turned 20 he was making a big-money move from Castres to Toulouse.

By then he had already been playing top-level club rugby for two years, having made his Castres debut in 2014. The following year he scored his first try for his club against Harlequins in the European Rugby Challenge Cup.

By 2016 he was starring at the World Rugby U20 Championship for France, scoring five tries, and full international recognition was only a matter of time away, coming in the 2017 Six Nations as he replaced Baptiste Serin in the win over Italy.

Since then he has become a fixture in the French squad, often as the replacement scrum-half but with the talent to make the position his own in years to come.

Toulouse sporting director Fabien Pelous said of Dupont: "Antoine is an explosive player, capable of breaking all defences but also to strategically lead his team through a game efficiently and with an excellent passing quality."

EPIC
MOMENTS

Our DHL team of international logistics specialists are proud to be working behind the scenes to deliver Rugby World Cup 2019™. We are playing our part to set the stage for players and fans to create memories that will last a lifetime!

Help us to identify the most breathtaking performances and match-winning plays by voting for the epic moments of the tournament.

To find out more, visit @DHLRugby and InMotion.dhl/EpicMoments

#RWCEpicMoments

RUGBY
WORLD CUP™
JAPAN日本2019

Official Logistics Partner

DHL

Wallabies

JACK DEMPSEY

The very fact Jack Dempsey has pulled on a gold jersey in recent times is testimony enough that the Sydney-born back-row is made of stern, and impressive, stuff.

After making his debut for Michael Cheika's Wallabies side in a 40-27 victory against Italy in June 2017, Dempsey seemed destined for a prolonged run in the starting XV and he soon rose to attention with a superb Man of the Match showing in a 23-18 win against New Zealand in October 2017.

However, a serious hamstring injury then cost Dempsey an entire year of his career as he struggled to regain his form and fitness. At one stage, questions were being asked about whether Dempsey could return at all yet he has proven the naysayers wrong and signed a new two-year deal with Rugby Australia late last year.

The NSW Waratahs star faces opposition for a starting place in Australia's back-row, especially with the likes of David Pocock and Michael Hooper being such class acts, yet recent performances have again underlined his foraging ability at the breakdown, his physicality and his endurance levels, and Dempsey is likely to be a star performer at RWC 2019.

STATS

Date of Birth: 12/04/1994
Height: 1.91m
Place of Birth: Sydney, Australia
Club: NSW Waratahs
Position: Back-row
Test Debut: v Italy, 2017

JOSH ADAMS

The rise and rise of Wales winger Josh Adams is illustrated perfectly by the fact he only made his international debut during his country's 2018 Six Nations campaign.

Aged 22, he was making such a positive impression with Worcester Warriors in the English Premiership that his claims could not be ignored. His form for his club meant a call-up by Wales coach Warren Gatland was inevitable.

Adams was handed his first international start against Scotland in February 2018 and by the following November he was lining up for Wales against Australia at the Principality Stadium as the home side ended a 13-match losing streak against the Wallabies. The previous year he had been in the stands watching the fixture as a fan!

He finished the 2017-18 Premiership season as joint-top try-scorer and was named in the end-of-season dream team.

Once part of the Wales set-up he made a big impression and his early caps will be best remembered for a fine individual try against Argentina in Santa Fe.

Adams had made the breakthrough as a professional with Llanelli before moving to Worcester in 2015.

He has signed for the Cardiff Blues ahead of the 2019-20 season and with his talent, speed and impressive side-step Adams could have a long and fruitful career in the Wales jersey.

STATS

Date of Birth: 21/04/1995
Height: 1.85m
Place of Birth: Swansea, Wales
Club: Cardiff Blues
Position: Winger
Test Debut: v Scotland, 2018

APHIWE DYANTYI

STATS

Date of Birth: 26/08/1994
Height: 1.83m
Place of Birth: Ngcobo, South Africa
Club: Lions
Position: Winger
Test Debut: v England, 2018

Aphiwe Dyantyi seems destined to be one of the stars of the show in Japan. Yet it seems remarkable to think that he may not even have been playing rugby at the moment, never mind starring at a Rugby World Cup, had he not rediscovered his love for the game while at the University of Johannesburg. It was while studying that Dyantyi again took up the sport he played so much as a child and his rise to prominence since then has been astounding, culminating in him being named the World Rugby Breakthrough Player of the Year 2018.

The Lions winger has pace and power in abundance but only made his South Africa debut in June last year in a narrow victory over England in Johannesburg. He scored a try on his debut, a further two shortly afterwards against Argentina and then a truly eye-catching brace against New Zealand as the Springboks recorded a superbly tense 36-34 win in Wellington. Dyantyi performed like a veteran that night rather than a young man playing just his seventh test match. In the time since then he has continued to improve and he could be one of the most exciting and explosive young talents on display at RWC 2019.

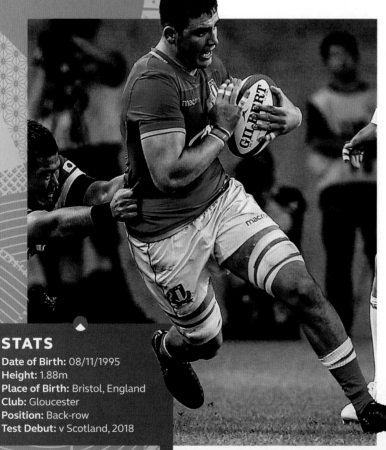

JAKE POLLEDRI

While no club has a crystal ball and can look into the future, officials at Bristol Rugby Club must take one look at Polledri and rue the day they let him pass.

Local boy Polledri looked a dead cert to sign for Bristol but they passed up on the offer and he has since gone on to thrive down the road at Gloucester.

And not only has Polledri proved his critics in Bristol wrong, he is also doing the same at international level.

Polledri qualifies for Italy through his grandmother Luisa and jumped at the chance to play for the country, beginning his international career at U20 level before breaking into the senior XV last year.

Polledri has earned huge plaudits at Gloucester for his endless energy and clear enjoyment of rugby's physical aspects yet he has become an increasingly effective ball carrier and his work-rate is also second-to-none. An ankle injury meant his 2019 Six Nations campaign was significantly curtailed and he now knows he is making up for lost time. Teams at RWC 2019 should beware – Polledri is back and he is hungry for success.

STATS

Date of Birth: 08/11/1995
Height: 1.88m
Place of Birth: Bristol, England
Club: Gloucester
Position: Back-row
Test Debut: v Scotland, 2018

SEMI RADRADRA

Numerous players have made their mark over the years having moved from rugby league to rugby union – and Semi Radradra is certainly doing that.

However, it was the 15-man game where he actually started playing as a youngster in his homeland, representing his nation at World Rugby U20 Championship 2011. Later that same year he also played for the Fiji sevens side in Dubai.

And it was there that he caught the eye of scouts from the Paramatta Eels rugby league side, learning the nuances of the 13-a-side game with their U20s and the Wentworthville Magpies.

By 2013 he was scoring tries for the Eels' first team and playing for Fiji in that year's Rugby League World Cup.

In 2014 he was on fire, scoring 19 tries in 24 matches for the Eels in the NRL competition and earning himself a bumper new contract.

He also switched allegiances to play for Australia in 2016 and the tries and moments of magic kept coming, earning him a big move to France to play rugby union with Toulon for the 2017-18 season.

In 2018 he moved to Bordeaux Bègles and earned his first Fiji cap against Georgia, and fittingly for such a flair player he scored a debut try from centre in a 37-15 victory.

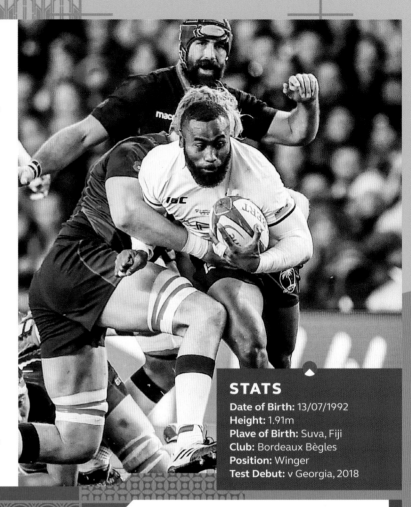

STATS

Date of Birth: 13/07/1992
Height: 1.91m
Plave of Birth: Suva, Fiji
Club: Bordeaux Bègles
Position: Winger
Test Debut: v Georgia, 2018

STATS

Date of Birth: 19/11/1995
Height: 1.70m
Place of Birth: Apia, Samoa
Club: Otago
Position: Scrum-half
Test Debut: v Scotland, 2017

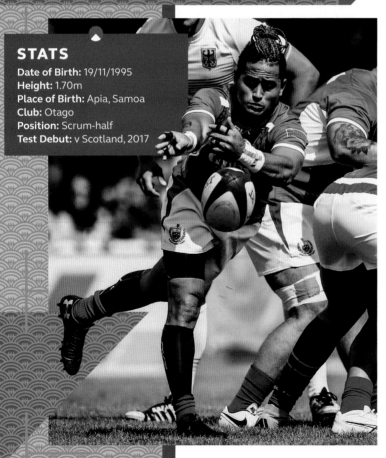

MELANI MATAVAO

Samoa have been well known for producing talented backs and Melani Matavao is the latest to really get supporters excited and up out of their seats.

The scrum-half burst onto the international scene during the November tests of 2017 when his country were touring Europe and now he has his sights set firmly on impressing at RWC 2019.

He has made big sacrifices to get to where he is now and quit working for the family business to try and make it as a professional player.

However, anyone who saw his cameo appearance off the bench on his Otago debut late in 2018 knows he has something about him and many believe he is the best attacking player to come out of Samoa for five or six years.

In July last year he helped his country qualify for Rugby World Cup 2019, scoring two tries in each match in the double header against Germany.

Samoa survived a scare in Heidelberg, scoring three tries in the last 11 minutes to confirm their place with a 42-28 second leg victory over the home side, meaning a 108-43 win on aggregate.

On their day Samoa can compete with anyone and Matavao will be a big part of that.

BAUTISTA DELGUY

Bautista Delguy is Argentina's latest find.

He only made his test debut against Wales in June 2018, but made an instant impact on the national team and has gone on from there.

He is slight and wiry but with ball in hand he really is lethal and playing for the Jaguares in Super Rugby has helped him get used to the rigours of top-level rugby and work out ways to find space against well-marshalled defences.

He has become one of the faces of the Argentinian renaissance and one of their most outrageous runners with ball in hand.

His greatest clips show him dropping a goal from the halfway line in a sevens match and he is always going forward except when he turns back to go forwards again. Attacks seem to become more dangerous when he gets his hands on the ball.

Before earning his full international call-up, he starred in the World Rugby U20 Championship in 2016, happy to go toe-to-toe, jink for jink with anyone that got in his way as his country won the bronze medal.

Having watched RWC 2015 on television as an 18-year-old, he is now ready to take the 2019 edition by storm.

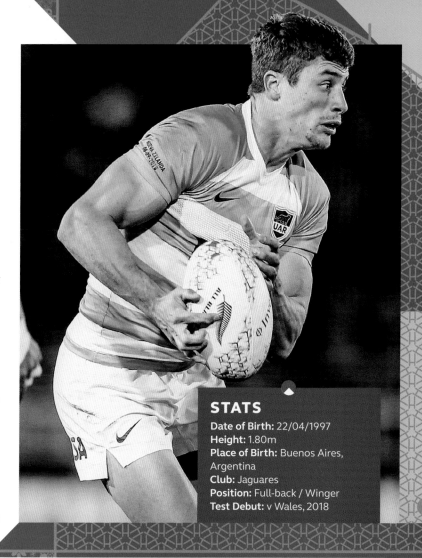

STATS

Date of Birth: 22/04/1997
Height: 1.80m
Place of Birth: Buenos Aires, Argentina
Club: Jaguares
Position: Full-back / Winger
Test Debut: v Wales, 2018

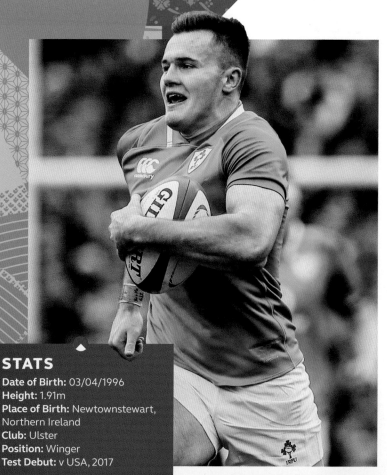

JACOB STOCKDALE

Even if Jacob Stockdale never pulled on the green shirt of Ireland again, it is fair to say he has already done enough to go down in folklore.

The 23-year-old may only be at the start of his international rugby adventure but he has made such an impression in his opening two years in an Ireland shirt that anything seems possible for the Ulster star.

Blessed with a muscular frame, an impressive turn of speed and that instinctive knowledge of being in the right place at the right time, Stockdale has come from nowhere to become one of Ireland's biggest attacking threats at RWC 2019.

He scored on his international debut against the USA in June 2017 and did not look back. November tries followed against South Africa and Argentina before Stockdale really hit top gear in the 2018 Six Nations, setting a new scoring record of seven tries in five matches as Ireland secured the Grand Slam and Stockdale was named Player of the Championship.

More glory was to follow in November 2018 when he scored the try that secured Ireland's first-ever victory against the All Blacks on home soil. Stockdale's future could not possibly look brighter.

STATS

Date of Birth: 03/04/1996
Height: 1.91m
Place of Birth: Newtownstewart, Northern Ireland
Club: Ulster
Position: Winger
Test Debut: v USA, 2017

ALL BLACKS®

BEAUDEN BARRETT

The relative merits of the world's top rugby players are always up for debate but anyone who has won the World Rugby Player of the Year award twice has earned a place among the greatest players ever to have graced the game.

That is the case for New Zealand's Beauden Barrett, who picked up the game's most prestigious individual award in 2016 and 2017, joining fellow All Blacks Dan Carter and Richie McCaw as the only players to have claimed the honour more than once.

His form and consistency mean no-one should be surprised to see Barrett at the top of the tree. He is one of the quickest fly-halves around, can play across the backline and at full-back, and he has a remarkable try-scoring record for his country.

The signs of an amazing career were there early. He holds the world record for the number of wins in a row from debut, having been involved in 19 consecutive victories following his first match as an All Black, an astonishing 60-0 win over Ireland in 2012.

His first Rugby World Cup, in 2015, saw him come away as a winner and he even came off the bench to claim a try in the 34-17 win over Australia in the final.

In a career full of highlights he also became the first player to score four tries against the Wallabies in one match during a 40-12 win in 2018.

STATS

Date of Birth: 27/05/1991
Height: 1.88m
Place of Birth: New Plymouth, New Zealand
Club: Hurricanes
Position: Fly-half
Test Debut: v Ireland, 2012

SCOTLAND

FINN RUSSELL

STATS

Date of Birth: 23/09/1992
Height: 1.83m
Place of Birth: Stirling, Scotland
Club: Racing 92
Position: Fly-half
Test Debut: v USA, 2014

Such is Finn Russell's maverick talent that it is no surprise that he grew up playing the sport with his brothers from a very young age.

A stonemason before he became a star with ball in hand, on the rugby pitch he helped Stirling County Colts win the under-18 National Youth Cup in 2011, and in 2013 it was announced he was a recipient of the MacPhail Scholarship and got the chance to travel to New Zealand.

He played club rugby for Falkirk and Ayr in Scotland and joined Glasgow Warriors in the pro ranks, having great success with them between 2012 and 2018, including winning the PRO12 title.

His exciting style of play and eye for a gap excited fans and Scotland called upon his talents for their June tour in 2014.

Then just 21, he earned his first cap under head coach Vern Cotter against the USA.

He started four of Scotland's five games at Rugby World Cup 2015 and, fast forward two years, he was a late call-up to the British and Irish Lions tour of New Zealand in 2017 along with Scotland team-mate Allan Dell.

A key man in Scotland's attack, the Racing 92 man has over 40 caps to his name already.

UAR

NICOLÁS SÁNCHEZ

Nicolás Sánchez is one of the most dangerous opponents in the game.

For proof of how good he is, just look at his points-scoring record. Aged just 29, he scored 14 points against New Zealand in 2018 to overtake Felipe Contepomi (651 points) at the top of Los Pumas' all-time scoring charts. And the worrying thing for anyone who wishes to overtake Sánchez in the future is that the fly-half has plenty more gas in the tank.

Contepomi was playing for Argentina beyond his 36th birthday. Using that yardstick, Sánchez could play at Rugby World Cup 2019 and still play for another five years to build up an imposing total.

His achievements shouldn't really be a surprise. Sánchez is a fly-half who has bags of ability and pace with the ball in hand.

The Stade Français star's threat was summed up at Rugby World Cup 2015 where he finished as the tournament's top points-scorer, ahead of the likes of Handré Pollard, Bernard Foley and Dan Carter. He has also consistently proved himself in The Rugby Championship, playing against New Zealand, Australia and South Africa, finishing top of the competition's scoring charts in 2014 and 2018.

STATS

Date of Birth: 26/10/1988
Height: 1.78m
Place of Birth: San Miguel de Tucaman, Argentina
Club: Stade Français
Position: Fly-half
Test Debut: v Uruguay, 2010

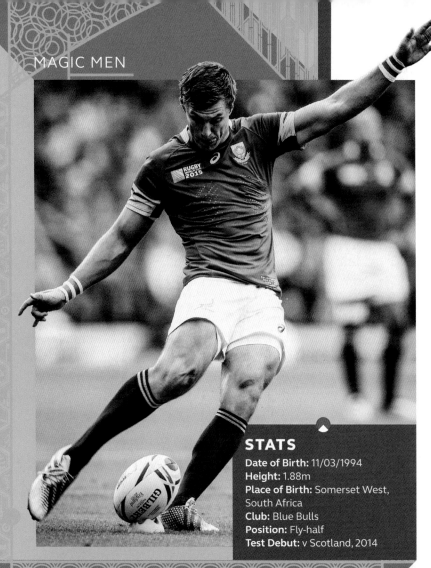

SPRINGBOKS

HANDRÉ POLLARD

Handré Pollard's pedigree as a young player meant he was always likely to become a star at the highest level of test rugby.

Before he made his test debut in 2014 he was already a big player for the Junior Springboks, particularly at the World Rugby U20 Championship 2012 where he scored 42 points to help South Africa win the tournament for the first time.

The following year he helped his team to the semi-finals and in 2014 – the year he was named Junior Player of the Year – he captained the side as they reached the final but lost out by just one point to England.

A senior call-up was inevitable and just eight days after that final Pollard joined Heyneke Meyer's senior squad, scoring 13 points on debut in a 55-6 win over Scotland.

Since then Pollard has regularly displayed his silky skills on the international stage.

His kicking is top drawer but his ability with the boot is matched by his brave running. He's not afraid to take on powerful opponents and has a two-try performance against New Zealand on his CV during a 27-25 win for the Boks in 2014.

STATS
Date of Birth: 11/03/1994
Height: 1.88m
Place of Birth: Somerset West, South Africa
Club: Blue Bulls
Position: Fly-half
Test Debut: v Scotland, 2014

RUGBY

DTH VAN DER MERWE

Rugby World Cup is a place for established star players to perform at their peak, but it can also be a platform for emerging players to make their names. That was the case for Canada's DTH van der Merwe.

In 2007 he earned a move to Saracens in England having impressed at the sport's showpiece occasion in France that year, scoring a try in an exciting draw between Canada and Japan.

Twelve years on and Van der Merwe is still a big threat on the world stage and a player his team-mates will look to for inspiration in Japan.

An intelligent winger, who can also play in the centre, he has tries in three consecutive Rugby World Cups, demonstrating his talent and longevity.

He also helped Canada reach the final of the Churchill Cup for the first time in 2010.

Since making his initial move to Saracens, Van der Merwe has forged an impressive career on the British Isles with Glasgow Warriors, Scarlets and Newcastle Falcons.

Club-level highlights include winning the PRO12 title with Glasgow in 2014 and the same title with Scarlets in 2017. Van der Merwe is also the leading try-scorer in Glasgow's history.

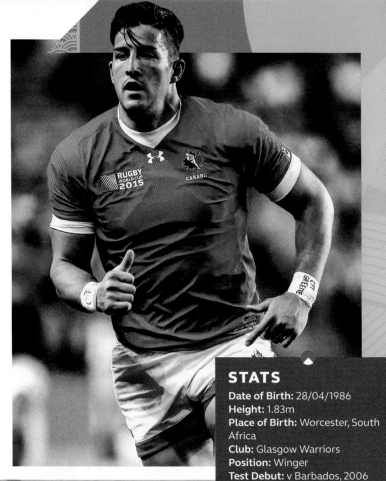

STATS
Date of Birth: 28/04/1986
Height: 1.83m
Place of Birth: Worcester, South Africa
Club: Glasgow Warriors
Position: Winger
Test Debut: v Barbados, 2006

FLYING FIJIANS

BEN VOLAVOLA

Whenever Ben Volavola is on the ball you think something is going to happen – and having already played at Rugby World Cup 2015 he is looking forward to another go at the showpiece event with Fiji.

Born in Australia to a Fijian mother, he is of Indian descent.

He spent many of his younger years in Fiji before returning to Australia in his teens, at which point his rugby career really took off.

A schoolboy star with Sydney's powerful Newington College, Volavola joined the NSW Waratahs at the start of the 2013 Super Rugby season and made his debut soon after.

He struggled to break into the team on a regular basis while there was a grand final defeat in the 2014 Shute Shield final with Southern Districts, before he joined the Crusaders and pledged his allegiance to Fiji when it came to the international arena.

More regular exposure with the Crusaders got him used to the rigours of being a fly-half at that level and since the months leading up to Rugby World Cup 2015 he has been the heartbeat of the Fiji team that always entertains whenever they get the chance.

He has also excelled in France with the star-studded Racing 92.

STATS

Date of Birth: 13/01/1991
Height: 1.91m
Place of Birth: Sydney, Australia
Club: Racing 92
Position: Fly-half
Test Debut: v Maori All Blacks, 2015

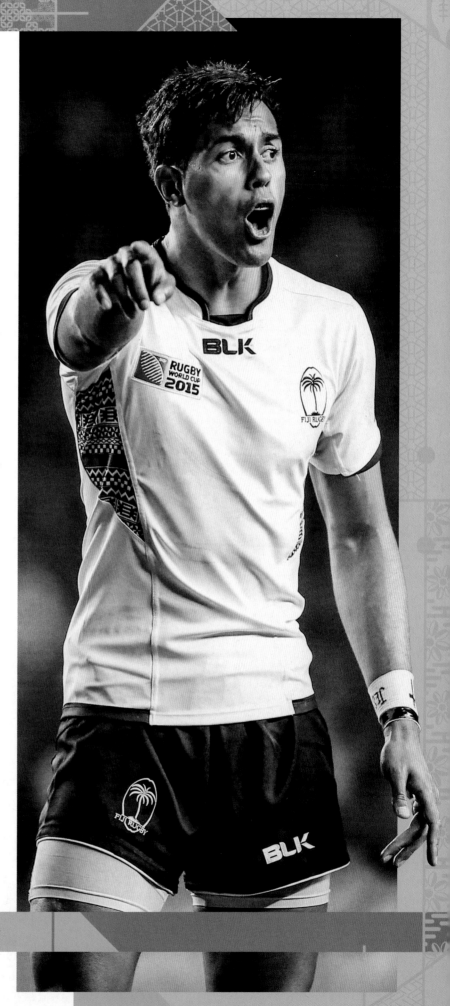

FELIPE
BERCHESI

Felipe Berchesi is one of those players who you can trust in the big moments.

All fly-halves that we are likely to see at Rugby World Cup 2019 will have that bit of stardust and although Uruguay are one of the underdogs Berchesi is certainly one to watch.

He began his career playing at home in Uruguay before playing for his country in sevens at the Pan American Games seemed to get him noticed abroad.

In 2013 he made the move to play in Italy with Rugby Badia, while in the same year the playmaker also represented his nation at Rugby World Cup Sevens in Moscow.

Since then he has been playing his club rugby in France, firstly with Chambery then Carcassonne, before the move to Dax in 2017.

And, in his early days with Dax, he showed his class, kicking 20 points and running the show as they saw off Colomiers 35-20.

In the international 15s game he made his Uruguay debut in 2011 against Portugal and has been a firm favourite of the fans ever since, having played at Rugby World Cup 2015 in the pool stage matches against Wales, Australia and England.

STATS

Date of Birth: 12/04/1991
Height: 1.80m
Place of Birth: Montevideo, Uruguay
Club: Dax
Position: Fly-half
Test Debut: v Portugal, 2011

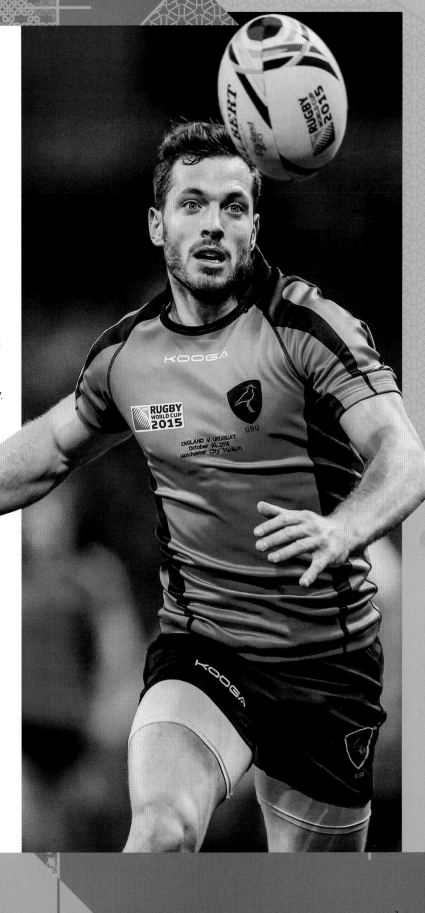

TUSI PISI

Longevity in rugby is hard to come by these days, but Samoan Tusi Pisi has made a pretty good job of it, playing at the top level for many years.

The secret to his extended career has probably been his versatility, the fly-half is also more than capable of playing in the centre or at full-back.

He was born in Samoa, but at a young age moved to Auckland in New Zealand with his family, including rugby playing brothers Ken and George.

After coming through the ranks at North Harbour and playing for New Zealand U21s, he hit the heights by playing for the Crusaders in Super Rugby and then his big break in Europe came when he joined Toulon in time for the 2007-08 season.

After two years in France he moved on to Japan to play for Suntory and the Sunwolves and in 2011, then aged 29 and after three caps for the Pacific Islanders in 2006, he made his Samoa debut against Japan.

Domestically he has since played for the Hurricanes in Super Rugby and Bristol Bears in England, while with his country he played a key part in their Rugby World Cup 2011 and 2015 campaigns.

STATS

Date of Birth: 18/06/1982
Height: 1.83m
Place of Birth: Apia, Samoa
Club: Toyota Industries Shuttles
Position: Fly-half
Test Debut: v Japan, 2011

CLIVEN LOUBSER

STATS
Date of Birth: 22/01/1997
Height: 1.75m
Place of Birth: Rehoboth, Namibia
Club: Welwitschias
Position: Fly-half
Test Debut: v Russia, 2017

Cliven Loubser was the hero in August 2018 as Namibia booked their place at Rugby World Cup 2019 with a 53-28 victory over Kenya.

It was always going to be a tough match in Windhoek, but they were determined to make it to their sixth successive showpiece event and young fly-half Loubser was on fire with 21 points to lead the way. That day he scored a late try to put the icing on the cake, while he also kicked five conversions and two penalties in what was one of the finest individual – and team – performances seen by Namibia in a long time.

It should not have come as a big surprise to those watching on that Loubser was at home in the pressure situation because earlier that same year, when they defeated Morocco 63-7 in Casablanca en route to winning the Rugby Africa Gold Cup, he had bagged 26 points, thanks to two well-taken tries and eight conversions. It was a one-sided affair, with the visitors superior to their opponents in every category, thanks mainly to the promptings of Loubser, who never looks flustered on the pitch and always remains calm under pressure, which are great traits to have when you are the playmaker in any team.

SOSO MATIASHVILI

Georgia have become known as a rugby nation that gets results when it matters – and Soso Matiashvili has built up a reputation as a man who scores spectacular tries on the big stage.

In 2017, in one of his earliest tests, the strong-running winger announced himself to the Georgian supporters and the wider rugby loving public with a superb score.

He takes up the story about a try that became an instant YouTube hit: "I saw there was a lot of space in behind their defence so, from full-back, I kicked ahead and then began the chase. The ball started to go into the dead ball area and I was saying 'don't go out, don't go out' and then I knew I had to jump to ground the ball before it went out and I was 100 per cent sure that I had grounded it."

Then, against Fiji the following year, Matiashvili was at it again.

As the ball came loose from a ruck he pinned his ears back, sprinted down the left wing before putting in a grubber to beat Penikolo Latu on halfway, controlling the bouncing ball with his left foot and then diving on it over the goal-line.

STATS
Date of Birth: 27/01/1993
Height: 1.80m
Place of Birth: Tbilisi, Georgia
Club: Rouen
Position: Full-back / Winger
Test Debut: v Spain, 2017

TOTO

Life Anew

https://www.toto.com

TOTOは、
ラグビーワールドカップ2019™
日本大会を応援します。

TOTO, supporters of Rugby World Cup 2019™

ALL BLACKS®

KIERAN READ

An outstanding international career will come to an end when New Zealand finish their Rugby World Cup 2019 campaign.

Kieran Read – one of only 20 men in history to win Rugby World Cup twice as a player – will retire from New Zealand duty at the end of this year's tournament, and whether or not he's able to lift the Webb Ellis Cup for a third time, the international game is losing one of its greats.

Read first pulled on an All Blacks jersey in 2008, making his debut in a win against Scotland, and his skill, athleticism and leadership saw him become one of the best number eights in the business.

That status was confirmed in 2013 when he was named World Rugby Player of the Year – two years after he had helped New Zealand to become world champions, a feat he achieved again in 2015.

When Richie McCaw stepped down as All Blacks captain after that triumph four years ago, Read was the natural choice to succeed him.

He may have been struck down with injuries in recent years but the Crusaders forward is still the leader of the pack for New Zealand and the leader of a team that will hope to clinch a third successive title.

STATS

Date of Birth: 26/10/1985
Height: 1.93m
Place of Birth: Papakura, New Zealand
Club: Crusaders
Position: Number eight
Test Debut: v Scotland, 2008

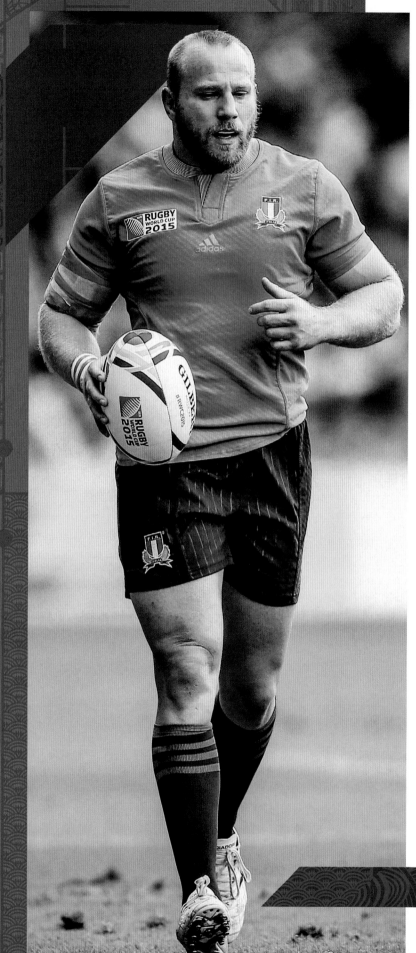

LEONARDO GHIRALDINI

Man for all seasons Leonardo Ghiraldini will have to use all his experience and expertise as he bids to help Italy reach the knockout stages of Rugby World Cup 2019.

Ghiraldini has played on the biggest stage at three different Rugby World Cups but will hope, at the age of 34, he and his Italian team-mates can make history by progressing beyond the pool stage.

Ghiraldini is known as a ball-carrying hooker and made the position his own soon after making his international debut in 2006.

In the 2011 Six Nations, he carried the ball more metres than any other hooker in the competition and he has also had the honour of captaining Italy during several spells, including throughout the 2010 Six Nations.

Ghiraldini's club career began in Italy with Petrarca Rugby before he moved to Calvisano where he won the Super 10. After that he had a five-year spell with Benetton Treviso before venturing abroad to sample English rugby with Leicester Tigers. He currently plies his trade in France with Top 14 champions Toulouse after moving there in 2016.

His potential as an international player was spotted early and he played for the Italian U18, U19 and U21 teams before playing for the Italy A team.

Since his test debut against Japan in 2006, Ghiraldini has taken some shifting from the side and he remains a key cog in the Italian machine.

STATS

Date of Birth: 26/12/1984
Height: 1.83m
Place of Birth: Padua, Italy
Club: Toulouse
Position: Hooker
Test Debut: v Japan, 2006

Russia

ANDREI GARBUZOV

Every team needs those tough as teak players who tackle everything that comes at them and always give 80 minutes of effort – and Andrei Garbuzov of Russia is certainly one of those.

You do not have a 14-year career at the top level without being a top performer and, all being well, Rugby World Cup 2019 will be his second showpiece event following on from 2011. Eight years ago Garbuzov played in four matches in New Zealand against USA, Italy, Ireland and Australia.

It took Garbuzov five test matches to score his first international try, against the Czech Republic in 2005, and it took until 2013 for him to win his 50th cap, a landmark that any player is proud to reach.

That 50th appearance was against Japan in Colwyn Bay in Wales, but sadly Russia went down in that one 40-13.

Russia finished fourth in the Rugby Europe Championship across 2017 and 2018, but were promoted to second after Romania and Spain were sanctioned for fielding ineligible players.

Head coach Lyn Jones said: "We've landed a hot-spot in the Rugby World Cup by default, so we've got a mountain to climb and I'll need my experienced players like Andrei to step up."

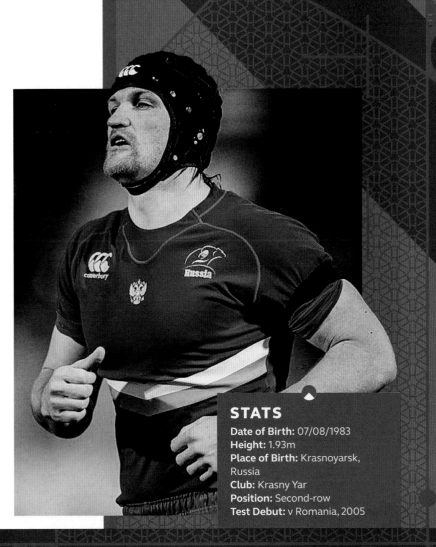

STATS
Date of Birth: 07/08/1983
Height: 1.93m
Place of Birth: Krasnoyarsk, Russia
Club: Krasny Yar
Position: Second-row
Test Debut: v Romania, 2005

MICHAEL LEITCH

Michael Leitch was born to lead and what an incredible job he makes of it. The New Zealand-born forward is the man his Japanese team-mates look to for leadership and Leitch, who was first named captain of the Brave Blossoms in 2014, always provides it.

Leitch moved to Japan when he was 15 to study and quickly became immersed in his new home's culture. By 2008 he was captaining Japan at the World Rugby U20 Championship and by 2013 he had claimed Japanese citizenship.

In 2011 Leitch gained his first experience of Rugby World Cup and played in all their pool matches, then at RWC 2015 he captained Japan to one of the biggest Rugby World Cup shocks ever as the Brave Blossoms toppled the mighty South Africa in their opening Pool B match.

Leitch isn't just a great leader though; he is also a great player. He is an expert around the breakdown and has scored many tries for Japan – including against South Africa and England.

Now in his 30s, his club career has taken him to Toshiba Brave Lupus in Japan's Top League, the Chiefs in New Zealand and Japanese Super Rugby team the Sunwolves.

STATS
Date of Birth: 07/10/1988
Height: 1.78m
Place of Birth: Christchurch, New Zealand
Club: Sunwolves
Position: Flanker
Test Debut: v USA, 2008

England Rugby

MARO ITOJE

Strength, speed, ability, leadership … Maro Itoje has it all.

If you were building the prototype of the ideal forward, indeed the ideal rugby player, you would end up creating someone similar to the Saracens star.

That is why, since his international debut for England in 2016, Itoje has been a fixture in Eddie Jones' side. But then, his progress through age-grade rugby always suggested he would have a future at the top of the game.

He represented England U18s and captained his team to victory at the World Rugby U20 Championship before also representing England Saxons.

Since then he has helped England to become Six Nations champions in 2016 and 2017 and started two of the British and Irish Lions' three tests against New Zealand in 2017.

At club level Itoje has shone. He made his debut for Saracens aged 19 and has gone on to win the Premiership four times and the European Rugby Champions Cup three times.

An intelligent player, who has studied for a politics degree, Itoje is recognised as one of the world's best players. With him in the side, England will always be a force to be reckoned with.

STATS

Date of Birth: 28/10/1994
Height: 1.96m
Place of Birth: Camden, London
Club: Saracens
Position: Second-row
Test Debut: v Italy, 2016

ALUN WYN JONES

Alun Wyn Jones has pretty much seen and done it all during a 13-year career as a Welsh international.

The Ospreys forward is one of the mainstays of the Wales team and a leader of the group.

With 125 caps under his belt after the Six Nations, the talismanic second-row will arrive in Japan on the verge of surpassing Gethin Jenkins as the most-capped Wales player.

It all started at international level for Jones in 2006 and by 2009 he had captained his beloved country for the first time.

His career has seen him star at three Rugby World Cups and take part in three British and Irish Lions tours. Jones ended the second of those tours (to Australia in 2013) as captain of the Lions in the deciding test. He has been a key component of four Six Nations successes for Wales, three of those with Grand Slams, including as captain in 2019.

For Ospreys, Jones – who has a degree in law – is an outstanding servant and in 2016 he broke the club record for the number of tries scored by a forward.

His standing in the game was confirmed in 2015 when he was nominated for the World Rugby Player of the Year award.

The only thing Jones hasn't achieved is to play in a Rugby World Cup final. Maybe this is his year.

STATS

Date of Birth: 19/09/1985
Height: 1.98m
Place of Birth: Swansea, Wales
Club: Ospreys
Position: Second-row
Test Debut: v Argentina, 2006

SPRINGBOKS

SIYA KOLISI

Siya Kolisi has blazed a trail for South Africa in recent times and not just because he is the first black South African to captain his nation.

Every international side on the planet would love to have Kolisi among its ranks.

Where to start with his qualities?

He is immensely strong, a powerful runner with the ball, a man who demands respect in the dressing room and out on the pitch and a man born to lead others into the physical world of test rugby.

Although versatile across the entire back-row, Kolisi comes into his own when playing as a flanker and his ability to steal opposition ball at the breakdown and be a generally disruptive influence to his opposite number ensures he is always in the heart of the action.

He became a Springbok the day before his 22nd birthday yet immediately looked at home. His preparations for RWC 2019 have been hit by a serious knee injury but his rehabilitation continues apace. His importance to the South African cause is absolute and Springboks fans are hoping he can return to lead in Japan in the same manner they have become accustomed to.

STATS

Date of Birth: 16/06/1991
Height: 1.88m
Plave of Birth: Zwide, South Africa
Club: Stormers
Position: Flanker
Test Debut: v Scotland, 2013

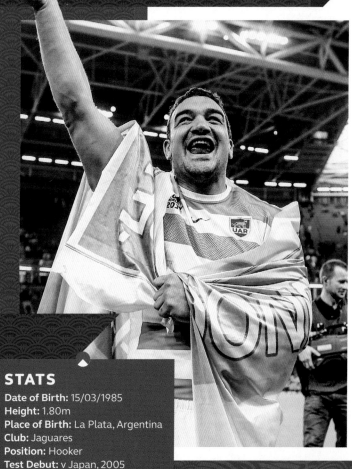

STATS

Date of Birth: 15/03/1985
Height: 1.80m
Place of Birth: La Plata, Argentina
Club: Jaguares
Position: Hooker
Test Debut: v Japan, 2005

UAR

AGUSTÍN CREEVY

The improvement of Argentina over the last decade or so has been one of rugby's most inspiring and interesting developments and Agustín Creevy deserves a fair share of the credit for helping Los Pumas evolve into one of the world's most exciting and difficult opponents.

Creevy started out as a flanker before moving to the front row with huge success. He was a fans' favourite at French club Montpellier where he earned the moniker 'Sonny Bill Creevy' in tribute to his superb handling and offloads and his compact size makes him a barrel of a man to try and tackle.

Creevy had an almighty tussle with Eusebio Guiñazú for the No.2 jersey for Argentina for a long time and although he did not always come off best, former Argentina head coach Daniel Hourcade clearly saw something he liked as he gave Creevy the captaincy in 2016.

His appointment came as a surprise to some but Creevy more than justified the armband and he has become one of the most respected elder statesmen on the international scene. A ferocious scrummager, he enjoys darting around the base of the pack and taking on all-comers. This is likely to be his last Rugby World Cup. He will want to remember it well.

FRANCE
RUGBY

LOUIS PICAMOLES

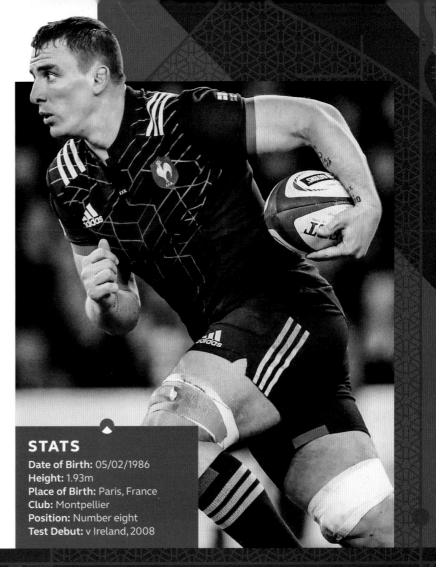

It takes a particularly tough kind of player – both physically and mentally – to withstand the rigours of 11 years of international rugby, especially if you make your living in the physical world of the back-row. However, France's Louis Picamoles has not only survived but thrived in that arena and goes into RWC 2019 as one of the most revered and respected forwards in the international game.

Picamoles is loved at Montpellier – he is in his second spell there following time at Toulouse and Northampton – and he is one of the players who will have to fire if France are to put a difficult 2019 to bed on a successful note.

The 2019 Six Nations did not live up to expectations but Picamoles, to his credit, never shirked the difficult questions nor sought to hide his disappointment at the way France had performed.

It is that level of honesty and commitment that the France squad should look to follow at RWC 2019. The 33-year-old is admired for more than his leadership skills though. Although not the tallest forward in the world, Picamoles is a wonder of a number eight, adept at hunting out turnovers, protecting his scrum-half and facing up to the toughest of physical challenges.

STATS

Date of Birth: 05/02/1986
Height: 1.93m
Place of Birth: Paris, France
Club: Montpellier
Position: Number eight
Test Debut: v Ireland, 2008

TONGA

STEVE MAFI

When rugby players talk highly about the qualities that their team-mates have on a regular basis then you know that the player in question is pretty special.

And if you take a look back through the archives you will find that team-mates of Tonga's Steve Mafi talk highly of him wherever he has been.

Former Leicester Tigers team-mate Dan Cole, for example, said: "Steve has the full range of gifts. He can run, he can jump, he can tackle like a ton of bricks, he's good in the tight phases, he can multi-task.

"He is very effective in everything that he does and he is a great influence on the team both on and off the pitch."

Mafi is the grandson of former Tonga captain Sione Mafi Pahulu and it is from that connection that he derives his pride of playing for his country.

He attended Westfields Sports High School in Australia and played his junior rugby at Parramatta Two Blues in Western Sydney. In 2007 he played for the Australian Schoolboys but in 2010 he switched allegiance, making his Tonga debut against old rivals Samoa.

Now with Castres in France, this war horse is just the kind of forward you want in your team.

STATS

Date of Birth: 09/12/1989
Height: 1.93m
Place of Birth: Fairfield, Australia
Club: Castres
Position: Second-row
Test Debut: v Samoa, 2010

URU

JUAN MANUEL GAMINARA

Anyone who has seen the video interview with Juan Manuel Gaminara straight after Uruguay qualified for Rugby World Cup 2019 cannot fail to be impressed by the passion that he has for playing for his country.

Uruguay qualified for RWC 2019 by beating Canada 32-31 in the second leg of their Americas 2 play-off to claim a 70-60 aggregate victory back in February 2018. Los Teros led the tie 38-29 after the first leg in Vancouver and went into the second game as firm favourites, but a much-improved effort from Canada had them rattled until Andrés Vilaseca crossed for the second time late on.

And a visibly emotional Gaminara said afterwards: "I am very happy for all of the guys in the squad, we are not a big rugby nation and we do not have a lot of players to pick from, but everyone works so hard for the team.

"We know that we have to give more than 100 per cent every time we pull on the jersey and we are very proud to play for Uruguay."

The pocket rocket back-row man has great memories of being at Rugby World Cup 2015 and he has been a key player for the national team since 2010.

STATS

Date of Birth: 01/05/1989
Height: 1.70m
Place of Birth: Montevideo, Uruguay
Club: Old Boys
Position: Back-row
Test Debut: v Romania, 2010

FLYING FIJIANS

LEONE NAKARAWA

Type in 'rugby offloads' to any internet search engine and you are sure to find this man sooner rather than later.

He has been wowing world crowds for a decade now since he made his test debut for Fiji against Tonga back in 2009 and the only surprise is that it took four years after that for a big European side to prise him away from his homeland.

By that time the athletic second-row had already made 19 appearances for his country and it was no surprise, given the flair with which he played the game himself, that it was then Glasgow Warriors head coach Gregor Townsend who took a chance on the big entertainer.

At the time Townsend, now the Scotland coach, stated: "He has played both 15s and sevens for Fiji and is a dynamic and skilful player. His ball carrying ability and versatility will really strengthen our squad, he can do things that others cannot."

He became a cult hero at Glasgow before joining Racing 92 in France in 2016 and in 2018 he was named European Player of the Year.

For his country he has appeared at the Rugby World Cup in both 2011 and 2015, and he also won an Olympic sevens gold medal at Rio 2016.

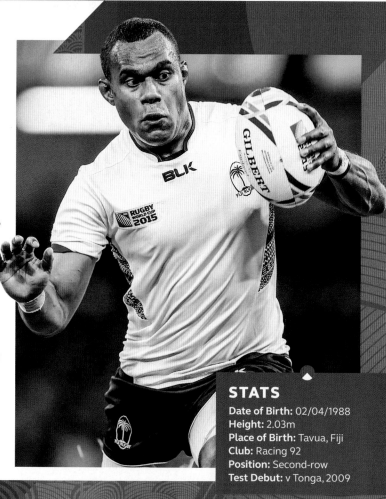

STATS

Date of Birth: 02/04/1988
Height: 2.03m
Place of Birth: Tavua, Fiji
Club: Racing 92
Position: Second-row
Test Debut: v Tonga, 2009

SECOM is an Official Sponsor of Rugby World Cup 2019™

SCOTLAND

GREIG LAIDLAW

As nephew of Scotland and British and Irish Lions legend Roy Laidlaw, Greig has top-quality international rugby running through his veins.

Just like his famous uncle, Greig mainly plays as a scrum-half, although he can operate at fly-half too.

The outstanding part of Laidlaw's game is his accurate kicking but he has the bravery and unpredictability which make him one of the best scrum-halves in the game.

He made his international debut in 2010, coming off the bench against New Zealand, and made his first start for his country in the 2012 Six Nations, scoring all 13 of Scotland's points against Wales.

Laidlaw hasn't looked back and he now has Chris Paterson's all-time Scotland record of 809 points in his sights, while he has already captained the Scots more times than any man in history.

His kicking has made him the hero for Scotland on many occasions. In 2013 Laidlaw's last-minute conversion clinched a 30-29 victory over Italy while he scored 26 points, including a late try, in a crucial 36-33 victory over Samoa at Rugby World Cup 2015.

A nomination for World Rugby Player of the Year award in 2015 illustrates the kind of company a world-class player like Laidlaw belongs in.

STATS

Date of Birth: 12/10/1985
Height: 1.75m
Place of Birth: Edinburgh, Scotland
Club: Clermont Auvergne
Position: Scrum-half
Test Debut: v New Zealand, 2010

IRFU

JOHNNY SEXTON

Ireland's Johnny Sexton is a rugby player who doesn't have any obvious weakness.

Tough in the tackle, superb at passing and a kicker with almost unparalleled accuracy, it's no wonder he was named the World Rugby Player of the Year in 2018. The only question is why it took so long for him to win it.

Sexton has been at the top of his game for around a decade.

A hero for both Leinster and Ireland, he kicks points for fun and is a natural leader. Indeed he is now Leinster captain and is one of Ireland's vice-captains.

It's his scoring rate that really grabs people's attention though. He is Leinster's top points-scorer of all time and is in the top 20 list of international points-scorers.

The clues about how prolific his boot is were there from the start. His first test came against Fiji in 2009 and saw him land 16 points with seven out of seven successful kicks. He's hardly missed one since.

He has been part of an Ireland squad that has won the Six Nations three times, including a Grand Slam in 2018, and has helped Leinster to four European Rugby Champions Cup wins.

STATS

Date of Birth: 11/07/1985
Height: 1.88m
Place of Birth: Dublin, Ireland
Club: Leinster
Position: Fly-half
Test Debut: v Fiji, 2009

OWEN FARRELL

England's Owen Farrell is one of the game's true global stars.

The Saracens points machine has won so much and performed so consistently throughout his career, and he should be in his prime at Rugby World Cup 2019.

Son of incoming Ireland head coach Andy Farrell, rugby is in Owen's blood and his knowledge of the game is demonstrated by the fact that he is world-class in two positions – fly-half and inside-centre.

It is his kicking that truly sets Farrell apart. He is deadly from any range and is already England's second-highest all-time points scorer.

His path to stardom began early and in 2008 he became the youngest player to appear in English rugby, 11 days after his 17th birthday, when he played for Saracens against Scarlets. He has gone on to have a glittering career for his club, winning the English Premiership title four times and the European Rugby Champions Cup twice. He was also named European Player of the Year in 2017.

On the international stage, since making his England debut in 2012 he has become one of his country's most important players and won the Six Nations twice as well as being nominated for the World Rugby Player of the Year award three times.

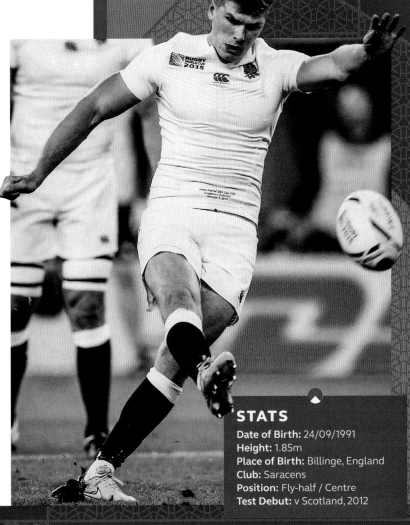

STATS

Date of Birth: 24/09/1991
Height: 1.85m
Place of Birth: Billinge, England
Club: Saracens
Position: Fly-half / Centre
Test Debut: v Scotland, 2012

Wallabies

DAVID POCOCK

David Pocock is widely regarded as one of the best forwards in the game.

Born in Zimbabwe, that's where he got his early rugby education before moving to Brisbane, Australia.

He worked his way up the age grades, representing Australia Schools, U19s, U20s, and then made his test debut in Hong Kong against New Zealand in 2008.

His rise from that point has continued, only interrupted by a few major knee injuries, and in both 2010 and 2011 his standing in the game was confirmed as Pocock was shortlisted for the World Rugby Player of the Year award.

His first Rugby World Cup, in 2011, saw him produce one of the great test performances as he helped inspire an 11-9 quarter-final win over holders South Africa, while in 2015 the combination of Pocock and Michael Hooper carried the Wallabies all the way to the final where the number eight scored a try but ultimately lost to New Zealand.

Pocock, who has also had the honour of captaining Australia, is known for his ability at the breakdown and his determination on the pitch is only matched by his strength of character off it, known for his charity work and campaigning on environmental and social issues.

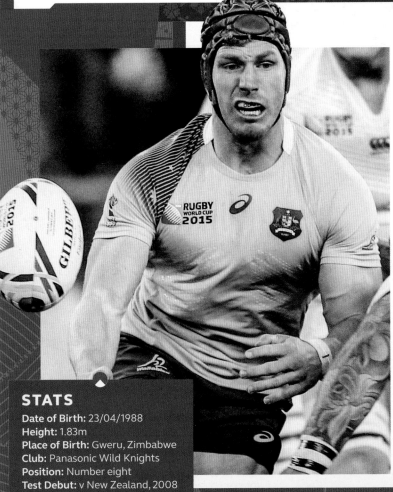

STATS

Date of Birth: 23/04/1988
Height: 1.83m
Place of Birth: Gweru, Zimbabwe
Club: Panasonic Wild Knights
Position: Number eight
Test Debut: v New Zealand, 2008

JOE TAUFETE'E

Having made his test debut for the USA at Rugby World Cup 2015, Joe Taufete'e is now looking to make his mark on the tournament in 2019.

He was born in American Samoa, but moved to America with his family when he was young and loved American Football whilst growing up.

A decent defensive tackle to College level, he suffered a serious knee injury that forced him to rethink his sporting future.

A spell in New Zealand was key as he tried to top up his rugby skills and he was a surprise pick in his country's Rugby World Cup 2015 squad.

He made his debut against South Africa in that event, though, and the hooker has not looked back.

Taufete'e equalled the world record of 15 tries by a front-row forward in international rugby in USA's 71-8 victory over Chile in their opening match of the Americas Rugby Championship in Santiago in February 2019.

Within a month he scored a hat-trick to break the record and shows no signs of stopping sniffing out the try-line.

Club-wise he has been in England since late 2016, becoming a key man for Worcester Warriors and, when he signed, was described as "hungry and talented" and "a very good forward" by then head coach Carl Hogg.

STATS

Date of Birth: 04/10/1992
Height: 1.83m
Place of Birth: Nu'uuli, American Samoa
Club: Worcester Warriors
Position: Hooker
Test Debut: v South Africa, 2015

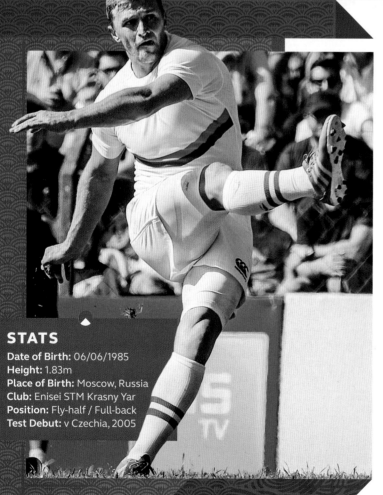

STATS

Date of Birth: 06/06/1985
Height: 1.83m
Place of Birth: Moscow, Russia
Club: Enisei STM Krasny Yar
Position: Fly-half / Full-back
Test Debut: v Czechia, 2005

Russia

YURY KUSHNAREV

Think of Russian rugby and you think automatically of the surname Kushnarev.

That is because George Kushnarev played flanker for the Soviet Union in the 1980s and then his sons Yury and Kirill began to play for Russia.

"I quite liked tennis as a youngster, but my father was a rugby player so I followed him and my older brother into rugby," Yury said.

"I started playing rugby as an 11-year-old and went professional after playing age group rugby."

In terms of club rugby Yury first played for VVA-Podmoskovye Monino, from 2003-04 to 2012-13, winning seven titles there, then for RC Kuban in 2013-14. Since then he has played for Enisei STM Krasny Yar.

However, it is on the international stage that he has really shown what he is all about. He starred for Russia at Rugby World Cup Sevens 2005 in Hong Kong and made his 15s debut later that year.

Now he has more than 100 caps for his country and has scored points galore for them.

In 2011 he was a member of the first Russian squad to compete at a Rugby World Cup, but he was also part of the group that failed to make it to the tournament in 2015 – so he cannot wait to be involved in Japan.

YU
TAMURA

STATS
Date of Birth: 09/01/1989
Height: 1.80m
Place of Birth: Aichi, Japan
Club: Sunwolves
Position: Fly-half
Test Debut: v Kazakhstan, 2012

Yu Tamura came off the bench to play his part in Japan's greatest ever result when they defeated South Africa 34-32 during the pool stage of Rugby World Cup 2015.

For every Japanese player it was the highlight of their international career and Tamura's had begun in the slightly less high profile surroundings of Almaty in Kazakhstan three years earlier.

Tamura scored a try from centre as the visitors easily defeated the hosts 87-0 and he has been in and around the Japan squad ever since.

At RWC 2015 he also started the pool match against Scotland in Gloucester and a year later he kicked 16 points in a 26-22 victory over Canada in Vancouver.

His 50th cap came in an impressive 28-0 win over Georgia in Aichi in June 2018, with the fly-half kicking 10 points to mark the occasion.

Given that Rugby World Cup 2019 is in his home country, Tamura, a strong tactical kicker, will be desperate to eclipse all of these memories in the tournament, and there is no doubt that he is one of the many Japanese players who have benefitted from playing regularly in Super Rugby with the Sunwolves.

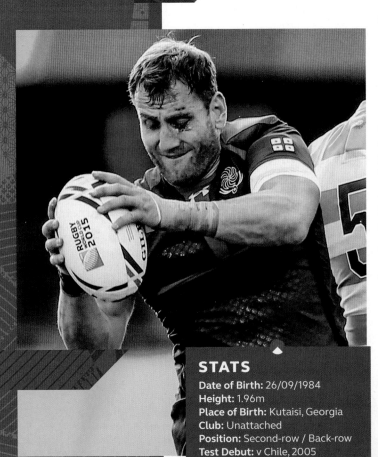

GIORGI
NEMSADZE

When you hear about talismanic players in national teams and are confused by the definition then you should look at Giorgi Nemsadze as a shining example of one.

He leads Georgia with such passion and carries the ball with such ferocity that there is no doubt he has been one of the driving forces to have helped push the nation to new heights.

He first played for the Georgian national side back in November 2005 against Chile. He missed out on Rugby World Cup 2007 selection, but he did not let that put him off.

In domestic rugby he played for a long time in France and represented clubs like Domont, Massy, Montauban, Agen and Tarbes before making the move to England in 2016.

Standing at 1.96m and weighing over 120kg, he moved to Bristol Bears at the time and then director of rugby Andy Robinson remarked: "Giorgi fits the bill for a Premiership lock. He's heavy, abrasive and he's been a key part of a Georgia forwards pack that has enjoyed considerable success."

Having played most recently in Wales for the Ospreys, he has represented his country at Rugby World Cup 2011 and 2015.

STATS
Date of Birth: 26/09/1984
Height: 1.96m
Place of Birth: Kutaisi, Georgia
Club: Unattached
Position: Second-row / Back-row
Test Debut: v Chile, 2005

BLAINE SCULLY

Scully is a natural sportsman – you just need to find out he was a star at basketball, water polo and swimming way back in high school to know that.

He eventually decided to move into a rugby career in college, where he immediately made an impact.

He won two National Championships with the University of California and made real waves at that level while he was also completing a degree in history.

His form was so good that, in the months leading up to Rugby World Cup 2011, he earned his first full cap for the USA against Russia.

He made four appearances at the showpiece event in New Zealand and in 2013 Leicester Tigers in England took a chance on him.

Given his leadership skills from his college days, it was no surprise that Scully was a solid vice-captain for the Eagles at Rugby World Cup 2015.

That same year the winger also joined Welsh side Cardiff Blues and, as well as becoming USA captain, he became a cult hero with the Welsh club's supporters, stating previously: "It is a true honour to put on the jersey and play in front of our great fans and passionate community."

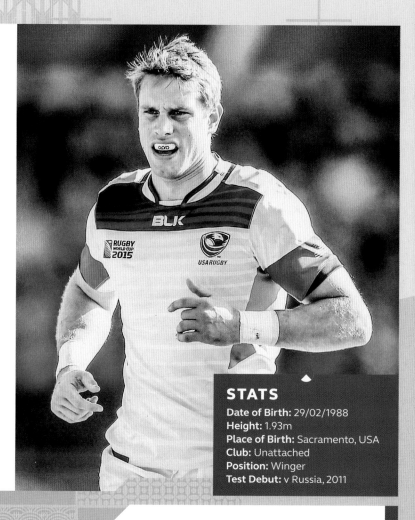

STATS

Date of Birth: 29/02/1988
Height: 1.93m
Place of Birth: Sacramento, USA
Club: Unattached
Position: Winger
Test Debut: v Russia, 2011

LESLEY KLIM

When Lesley Klim scored four tries for Namibia against Tunisia in June 2018 his career really had taken off for club and country.

Having been capped by his country throughout the age grades and in sevens, he made his senior international debut against Spain in June 2017 in the World Rugby Nations Cup in Uruguay.

During that time he was also featuring regularly for Windhoek-based side Welwitschias in South Africa's domestic competition the Currie Cup, finishing two seasons as his club's top try scorer.

That eye-catching form for club and country saw him handed the chance to move to the UK at the turn of 2018, joining Doncaster Knights on a short-term contract.

There are ways to make your mark and then there are ways to really make your mark and a try-scoring man of the match debut against Bristol in mid-January of that year was the latter.

That performance really set tongues wagging and he was snapped up by Welsh PRO14 side Ospreys ahead of the 2018-19 season.

Klim loves to run with the ball but is equally adept at creating space and chances for others. Either way, this ultimate team player will be a real threat in Japan.

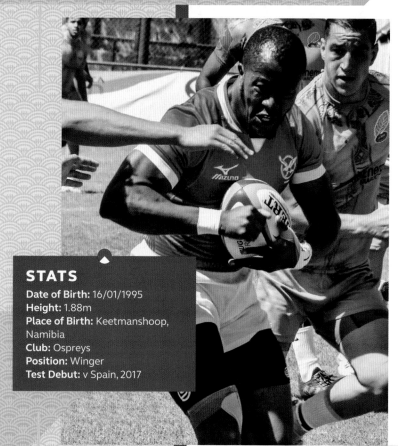

STATS

Date of Birth: 16/01/1995
Height: 1.88m
Place of Birth: Keetmanshoop, Namibia
Club: Ospreys
Position: Winger
Test Debut: v Spain, 2017

ALL BLACKS

RIEKO IOANE

There can be few more daunting sights for a full-back in international rugby than that of Rieko Ioane, in full flow, running towards you.

The 22-year-old is very much the epitome of the archetypal modern player. Tall, strong, incredibly fast, aggressive in both attack and defence; there is nothing that Ioane cannot do and he has become a wonderful addition to New Zealand's array of talents in recent years.

He caught the eye of Steve Hansen after starring for the All Blacks Sevens and since making his 15s debut against Italy in November 2016, he has not looked back and was named World Rugby Breakthrough Player of the Year in 2017.

As the brother of fellow New Zealand international Akira and the son of former Samoan player Eddie, rugby is well and truly in Ioane's blood and after becoming the eighth-youngest All Black in history, Ioane has more than proved his worth at the highest level.

If he can remain fit and healthy, and if he can maintain his current superb scoring rate, Doug Howlett's all-time record of 49 tries for the All Blacks may well one day be overtaken by the young man from Auckland.

STATS

Date of Birth: 18/03/1997
Height: 1.88m
Place of birth: Auckland, New Zealand
Club: Blues
Position: Winger
Test Debut: v Italy, 2016

FLYING FIJIANS

VERENIKI GONEVA

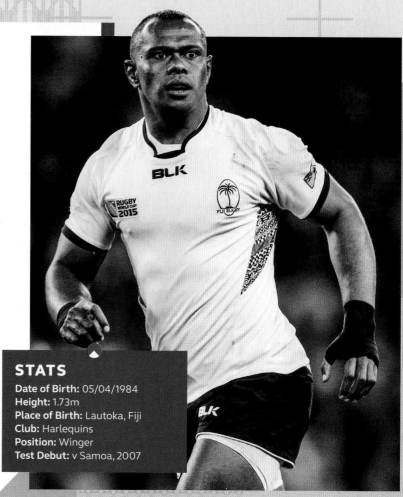

Vereniki Goneva is, quite simply, a legend of Fijian rugby, whose mixture of pace and power has made him one of the most feared attackers in the game.

Goneva signed for Newcastle Falcons in 2016 after scoring 44 tries in 94 outings for Leicester Tigers. His spell at Leicester included a try on debut against London Welsh, scoring in the Premiership final victory over Nothampton as the Tigers clinched the league title in 2012-13, and taking the Premiership's top try-scorer award for 2013-14, in the process winning the vote of his peers as the Rugby Players' Association Player of the Year. He was also shortlisted for European Player of the Season in 2015-16 after touching down six times in the Champions Cup. Since joining Newcastle, the tries and the accolades have kept coming, winning Premiership Player of the Year in 2017-18 after a blistering 13 tries in 19 appearances.

A devastating strike runner, Goneva's international career has been similarly prolific, with 20 tries in 55 appearances so far. His eight Rugby World Cup appearances have yielded five tries, having appeared in both 2011 and 2015, and 2018 was notable for his spearheading of Fiji's successful push for a fourth Pacific Nations Cup title.

STATS

Date of Birth: 05/04/1984
Height: 1.73m
Place of Birth: Lautoka, Fiji
Club: Harlequins
Position: Winger
Test Debut: v Samoa, 2007

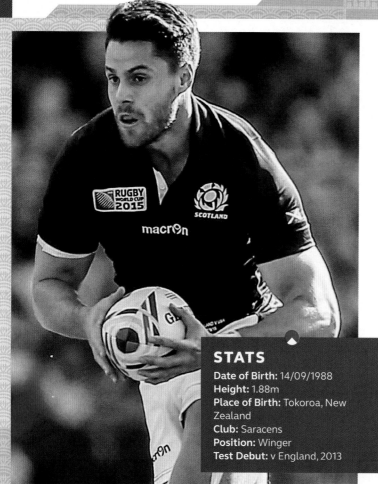

SCOTLAND

SEAN MAITLAND

Growing up in New Zealand, Sean Maitland may not have envisaged becoming a Scotland stalwart when he was older, but that is the way things have turned out.

It was some 12 years ago that Maitland began to hit the headlines in New Zealand when he played an integral role in their U19 World Championship success, following it up a year later with the U20 crown.

After helping the Crusaders to the Super Rugby title in 2008, a number of injuries came along but a four-try haul against the Brumbies in March 2011 showed he was still a danger, and the Crusaders made another final.

With two grandparents born in Glasgow he made the move to the northern hemisphere in 2012, joining the Warriors, and he made his Scotland debut against England in the 2013 Six Nations at Twickenham. A wing spot in navy blue soon became his on a regular basis.

At Rugby World Cup 2015 he featured in four of Scotland's five games, including their quarter-final defeat by Australia, a result that frustrated him given that his cousin is Quade Cooper!

He now plays for English side Saracens.

STATS

Date of Birth: 14/09/1988
Height: 1.88m
Place of Birth: Tokoroa, New Zealand
Club: Saracens
Position: Winger
Test Debut: v England, 2013

GEORGE NORTH

Everyone loves to watch a powerful winger in full flow and when George North gets going for Wales he is most certainly that.

In fact, it is amazing to think that he is still only 27, given that he played at Rugby World Cup 2011 and the showpiece event in 2015 and has been on two British and Irish Lions tours.

He was born in England, but grew up in Wales having moved to Anglesey when he was two, and he is a Welsh speaker.

His professional rugby career began at the Scarlets and he was first called up by his country for the November tests in 2010.

He scored two tries on his international debut against South Africa in Cardiff as the hosts were edged out 29-25, but everyone who watched him that day knew he was a quality player.

As he was only 18 at the time he became the youngest player to ever score a try on his Wales debut and there was plenty more where that came from.

As well as this year's Grand Slam, North played his part in Wales' victorious Six Nations campaigns in 2012 and 2013, while club-wise he has since played for Northampton Saints in England and the Ospreys back in Wales.

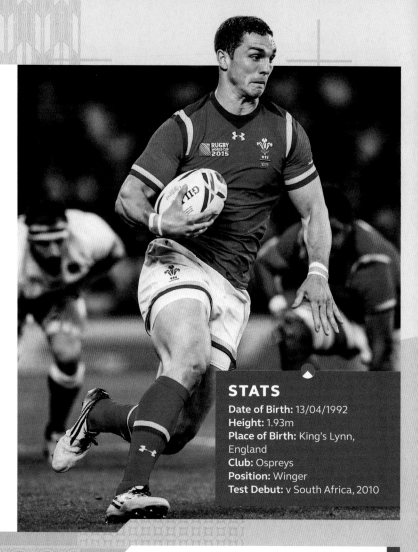

STATS
Date of Birth: 13/04/1992
Height: 1.93m
Place of Birth: King's Lynn, England
Club: Ospreys
Position: Winger
Test Debut: v South Africa, 2010

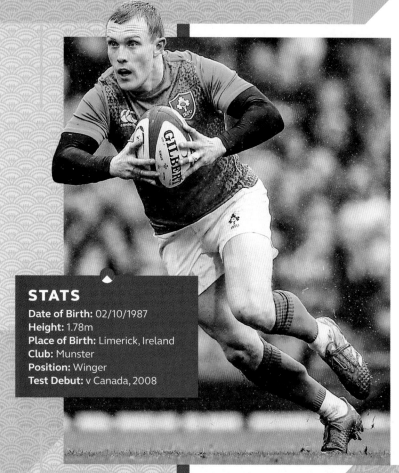

KEITH EARLS

Irish speed king Keith Earls will be looking to add to his record tally of Rugby World Cup tries when he takes part in his third tournament.

Earls surpassed Brian O'Driscoll's Irish record of tries at Rugby World Cups when he crossed against Italy in 2015 to score his eighth, including the five he scored in New Zealand in 2011.

Now in his early 30s, there is still plenty more to come from the Munster man who predominantly plays on the wing, but can also be utilised at centre or full-back. With a bit of luck and depending on selection, he might even threaten the overall record of 15 Rugby World Cup tries held by Bryan Habana and Jonah Lomu.

Earls made his Ireland debut back in 2008 against Canada and his golden touch was very much in evidence straight away as he scored with his first touch of the ball. He is now one of the most experienced players in the squad.

He was part of the Ireland team that won the Six Nations Grand Slam in 2018 and was also part of the British and Irish Lions squad that toured South Africa in 2009.

With Munster he has won the PRO14 twice and also the European Rugby Champions Cup in 2008.

STATS
Date of Birth: 02/10/1987
Height: 1.78m
Place of Birth: Limerick, Ireland
Club: Munster
Position: Winger
Test Debut: v Canada, 2008

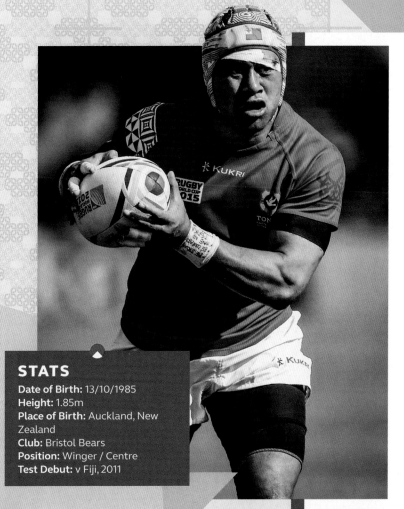

TONGA

SIALE PIUTAU

His younger brother Charles may have played for New Zealand between 2013 and 2015, but it has been with Tonga that Siale Piutau has made his mark on the world stage over the years.

Having been born in Auckland, New Zealand, he joined Counties Manukau during the 2006 season.

Lining up next to former All Black Tana Umaga in midfield, he was named the 2010 Counties Manukau Player of the Year.

That kind of form helped him force his way into Super Rugby reckoning and he was part of the Chiefs' wider training group in 2010.

He made his debut that season before joining the Highlanders in 2011, staying there for two years before a new adventure in Japan with Yamaha Júbilo.

Since 2016 he has been in England with Wasps and now the Bristol Bears, and on the international stage he has been playing for Tonga since 2011.

He played two tests against Fiji in August of that year and then made the squad for Rugby World Cup 2011, becoming a key member of the side and scoring two tries against Canada.

Since that New Zealand tournament he has been a mainstay of the Tonga side and has also captained the team, and he played in four matches at Rugby World Cup 2015.

STATS

Date of Birth: 13/10/1985
Height: 1.85m
Place of Birth: Auckland, New Zealand
Club: Bristol Bears
Position: Winger / Centre
Test Debut: v Fiji, 2011

SPRINGBOKS

S'BUSISO NKOSI

Yes, S'Busiso Nkosi is young.

Yes, S'Busiso Nkosi is raw and inexperienced.

But, so far, all the signs are there that he is going to become one of the Springboks' most lethal weapons in the years to come. While most commentators tend to see a lack of international experience as a negative, in the case of Nkosi it is no such thing because he is so keen, so fearless and so unscathed precisely because he carries little painful baggage over the defeats of yesteryear.

His double try-scoring debut against England in Johannesburg in June 2018 is a case in point.

South Africa somehow recovered from 24-3 down to pip Eddie Jones' side 42-39 in one of the most exciting, tumultuous and interesting test matches of the year.

Nkosi started that occasion – after several years of being noted as The Next Big Thing – yet rather than let the expectations affect his performance, he was a stand-out Springbok on an afternoon where everybody shone. He has gone from strength to strength since that encounter and as he hones his match smarts and continues to improve his pace, Nkosi is going to be dynamite to watch – and to play with.

STATS

Date of Birth: 21/01/1996
Height: 1.80m
Place of Birth: Barbeton, South Africa
Club: Sharks
Position: Winger
Test Debut: v England, 2018

England Rugby

JONNY MAY

There are quick players and then there is Jonny May.

Everyone knows that in the modern game space is hard to come by with defences so well organised, but for club and country May seems to find the gaps, and he is the master of creating something out of nothing with his pace and power.

He broke through into the pro ranks at Gloucester a decade ago and since then he has wowed crowds and scored many tries.

In terms of England, he went on his first international tour to South Africa in 2012 and although not capped on that occasion he impressed midweek against the Sharks.

And it was not long until his test debut came, in the second match of the following year's tour to Argentina, which England won comfortably.

He had to wait a while for his first try at the top level, coming in November 2014 and since then he has been one of England's most prolific marksmen.

May now plays his club rugby for Leicester Tigers and having played in Rugby World Cup 2015 he will be eager to fire England to glory in this year's showpiece event under the watchful eye of Eddie Jones.

STATS

Date of Birth: 01/04/1990
Height: 1.88m
Place of Birth: Swindon, England
Club: Leicester Tigers
Position: Winger
Test Debut: v Argentina, 2013

NEC.
YOUR PUBLIC SAFETY PARTNER.

Peaceful urban scenes hide sophisticated safety solutions

Safety in the city is one of the greatest needs today. That is why NEC works 24/7, designing and installing modern technological solutions to increase your safety and quality of life in various cities around the world. Count on NEC's public safety solutions for a more protected, safe and brighter society.

NEC is an official sponsor of Rugby World Cup 2019™

www.nec.com/rwc2019

JAPAN EMBRACES

It's one thing hosting a Rugby World Cup, it's quite another taking the tournament to your heart

Back in July 2009, World Rugby convened a special meeting in Dublin in which the 26-man Council voted for Japan to be the hosts of Rugby World Cup 2019.

At the time, Japan Rugby Football Union chairman Nobby Mashimo said: "This is a special bid as it is a bid for rugby in Asia.

"With the support of our friends from all 26 unions in the region, and the backing of the Japanese government and business community, we believe that we can deliver a Rugby World Cup that will capture the hearts and minds of people and provide the platform to take rugby to new levels in Asia. We welcome the expansion of the game into a new frontier."

> "It's incredibly exciting to see the phenomenal response from rugby fans here in Japan and from across the world"

They are noble words, and noble intentions, from Mashimo but not even he could have dreamt that Japan would embrace RWC 2019 in quite the manner it has done.

Put simply, the world of rugby has never seen excitement like it.

From fan engagement, legacy, tickets sold and column inches written, RWC 2019 has been well and truly embraced in Japan.

When tickets first became available in the initial ballot phase, more than 4.5 million applications were made by over 300,000 spectators as they bid to get those priceless spots in the 12 different stadiums that will host games later this year.

In January this year, a further 200,000 tickets went on general sale and were also snapped up in no time at all. Proof, if it were needed, that not only has Japan welcomed RWC 2019, it has well and truly taken it to its heart.

"It's incredibly exciting to see the phenomenal response from rugby fans here in Japan and from across the world," Japan 2019 Organising Committee CEO Akira Shimazu said.

"The huge demand for tickets points to Rugby World Cup 2019 being a truly special tournament.

"Rugby World Cup 2019 will be a once-in-a-lifetime experience for the people of Japan and for rugby fans from across the world.

"Hosting Asia's first Rugby World Cup is a dream come true for millions of Japanese rugby fans and a wonderful opportunity to showcase Japan to the worldwide rugby community."

Tickets for all of Japan's matches sold out instantly, as did every seat available for the games in the knockout stages.

In addition to that, 13,000 volunteers have been selected to help out at the tournament – 3,000 more than anticipated out of a pool of 38,000 applicants – and that also underlines just how excited Japan is about the upcoming tournament.

"The response we received for our 'Team No-Side' volunteer programme has been simply incredible in terms of the 38,000 applications," Shimazu added.

"The enthusiasm and passion shown by those who have gone through to the interview stages has been really encouraging. Our volunteers will be superb ambassadors for both rugby and Japan, welcoming domestic and international fans to this once-in-a-lifetime Rugby World Cup. I extend my sincerest gratitude to all of them."

Yet just as important as crammed stadia and delighted fans from across the globe is the long-lasting impact RWC 2019 will have on the next generation of rugby supporters in Japan and across Asia.

In 2013, World Rugby launched the Impact Beyond programme to help rugby continue its astonishing

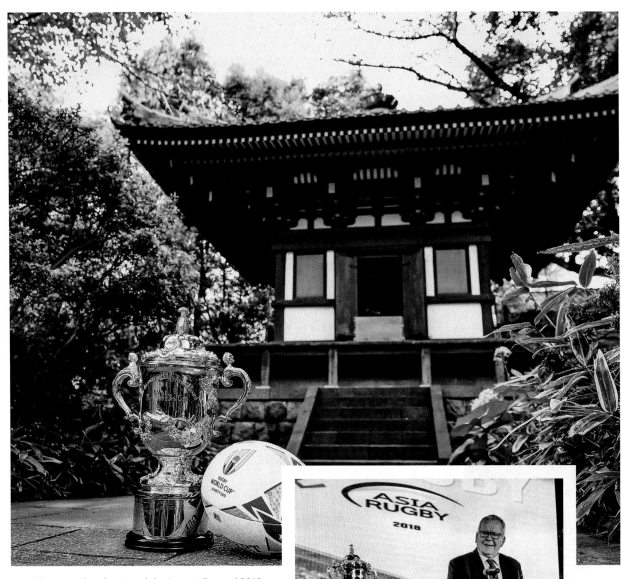

growth across the planet and the Impact Beyond 2019 scheme has concentrated on Asia – with amazing results.

In the run-up to RWC 2019, over 460,000 Japanese participants have got involved in the game and across the Asian continent, the tournament has been the catalyst for an incredible one million new rugby players.

"We want to grow the game on what is sure to be an extremely successful Rugby World Cup," World Rugby Chairman Sir Bill Beaumont said.

"Japan 2019 is shaping up to be World Rugby's most successful legacy programme to date. Creating a sustainable legacy is a central pillar in our major event planning and delivering a tangible, long-term impact beyond the six-week event is critical to the event's success. Inspiring interest in rugby across Asia was one of the core reasons for bringing the Rugby World Cup to Japan.

"It is a truly exciting time for rugby in Asia with fan engagement, broadcast audiences and player participation numbers growing year-on-year.

"Our gratitude and appreciation goes to the many thousands of volunteers who regularly give their time to support Impact Beyond programmes on the ground. They are the unsung heroes of Rugby World Cup 2019."

More tickets sold, more volunteers found, more new players created – Japan really is ready, willing and able to embrace a Rugby World Cup like never before.

> "It is a truly exciting time for rugby in Asia with fan engagement, broadcast audiences and player participation numbers growing year-on-year"

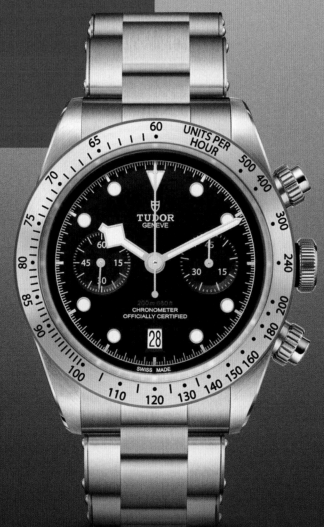

RUGBY
WORLD CUP™
JAPAN 日本 2019
TOURNAMENT SUPPLIER

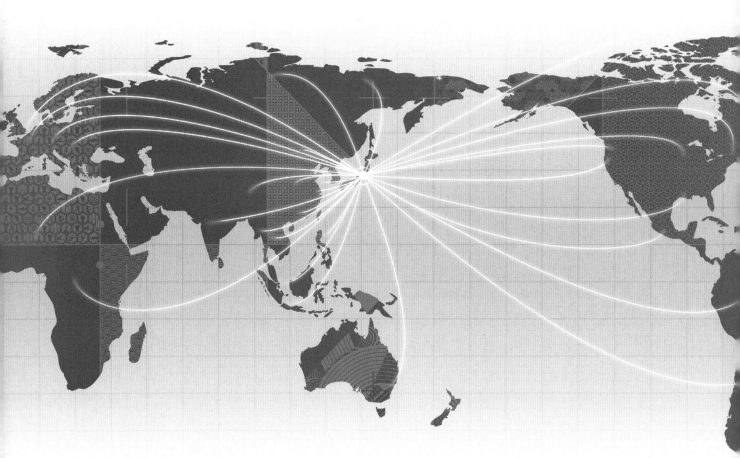

TOPPAN

Blueprint for Success

As a global leader on our field, Toppan is proud to support Rugby World Cup 2019.™
Printing, packaging, security solutions—our team can put your team on the path to winning.

www.toppan.com

POOL A

After a blistering few years in which they beat the All Blacks twice, won a series in Australia for the first time and a Six Nations Grand Slam in 2018, Ireland's status as northern hemisphere favourites for Rugby World Cup 2019 took a slight hit after a flat Six Nations campaign earlier this year. Defeats to England and Wales raised the question of whether they had peaked too soon, but they are still ranked third in the world and with their strength and physicality, their peerless kicking game and Johnny Sexton leading the way, they remain huge favourites to top Pool A.

Ireland's opening match against Scotland could be the decisive game of the pool, however, with the winner likely to avoid the All Blacks in the quarter-finals – surely enough of a motivation to make it a pulsating contest. Scotland have had an upturn in fortunes under the stewardship of Gregor Townsend, running New Zealand close in 2017 and beating England in the Six Nations for the first time in a decade, in 2018. Always solid at home, Scotland often flatter to deceive away from Murrayfield, but the experience of coming within 30 seconds of upsetting Australia at Rugby World Cup 2015 and a thrilling 38-38 draw with England in this year's Six Nations, recovering from 31-7 down at half-time to almost snatch a famous victory, means Rugby World Cup 2019 could be the tournament Scotland finally turn promise into results.

What makes Pool A so intriguing, though, is the presence of the hosts, Japan. They sent shockwaves through the sport at Rugby World Cup 2015, producing perhaps the biggest upset in the tournament's history when they beat South Africa 34-32 in Brighton, and while their current squad may not be as strong as that 2015 version, climate familiarity and a vociferous home support could ruffle a few feathers. Japan lost only once at Rugby World Cup 2015 and have had unprecedented access to tier one nations since then, including a notable win over Italy and a draw with France. Their pool games finish against Scotland, and Jamie Joseph's men will hope they are still in contention for the quarter-finals.

To do that, though, the Brave Blossoms will need to get off to a good start against Russia, who they only just managed to beat last November, winning 32-27 after trailing 22-10 at half-time. Coached by the former Wales flanker Lyn Jones, Russia had a mixed 2018, beating Canada and Namibia but conceding 62 points to the USA. It's been more of the same in 2019, but the Bears performed with credit in their previous Rugby World Cup appearance in 2011 and they will be happy to produce similar efforts in Japan.

Meanwhile, everyone's favourite giant killers Samoa often draw plaudits for their attacking style of play, and they will be taking a strong squad keen to make their mark after disappointing in their last two Rugby World Cups.

IRELAND

STAR MAN

JOHNNY SEXTON

Filling the fly-half void left by Ireland great Ronan O'Gara might have been too big a job for some players. But Sexton is not one of them. The Leinster star has become Ireland's fulcrum in recent years, his effortless and intelligent kicking game matched by his bravery, passing vision and willingness to sacrifice himself for the Ireland cause. Sexton's talent helped him seal the World Rugby Player of the Year 2018 accolade, just the second Irishman to win the award after Keith Wood in 2001. Wood, rightly, has gone down in Ireland's history as one of their finest ever players. Sexton deserves the same plaudits.

COACH

JOE SCHMIDT

Joe Schmidt is a tough coach who knows how to get the best from his Ireland side. After replacing Declan Kidney in April 2013, he won back-to-back Six Nations titles and has taken Ireland as high as number two in the World Rugby Rankings. A quarter-final loss to Argentina punctured their RWC 2015 hopes but the 2018 Six Nations Grand Slam plus two wins over New Zealand – Ireland's first ever successes against the All Blacks – have elevated Schmidt in the eyes of Ireland supporters. Andy Farrell replaces him as Ireland head coach after RWC 2019 and Schmidt will head into retirement as a widely respected and admired strategist.

IRELAND
SCOTLAND
JAPAN
RUSSIA
SAMOA

POOL A

IRELAND
RUGBY WORLD CUP STATISTICS

World Ranking*	RWC Titles	RWC Apps
3	0	8

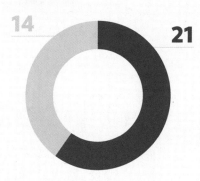

35 MATCHES PLAYED

14

21

● Won   ● Lost   ● Drawn

Points scored:	Tries scored:
973	116

Average per match:	Average per match:
27.80	3.3

Conversions:	Penalties:	Drop goals:
88	76	9

Red cards:	Yellow cards:
0	5

POOL A FIXTURES

SCOTLAND
Sun 22 Sep, 16:45
International Stadium
Yokohama

JAPAN
Sat 28 Sep, 16:15
Shizuoka Stadium
Ecopa

RUSSIA
Thurs 03 Oct, 19:15
Kobe Misaki
Stadium

SAMOA
Sat 12 Oct, 19:45
Fukuoka Hakatanomori
Stadium

All world rankings correct as at end of June 2019

OVERVIEW

After winning back-to-back Rugby World Cups, New Zealand will arrive in Japan with plenty to look forward to, knowing they have the mettle and game to beat most sides.

So it is a huge credit to Ireland that New Zealand will be hoping to avoid them at Rugby World Cup 2019 thanks to the huge steps they have made under, ironically enough, Kiwi Joe Schmidt.

Wales might be the Six Nations Grand Slam winners but the tussle to be labelled the best team from the northern hemisphere is a close-fought battle between Warren Gatland's side and Ireland due to the beautifully balanced and solid team Schmidt has developed in recent years.

Led by the streetwise Rory Best, Ireland can beat you doggedly or with real flair.

Best heads up a pack full of huge men and huge talent.

Indeed, while Ireland legend Paul O'Connell's retirement was always going to leave a mighty gap to fill, Ireland have more than managed in his absence.

A scrum containing the likes of CJ Stander, Devin Toner, Peter O'Mahony, Tadhg Furlong and Cian Healy means serious business, providing plenty of muscle and ball for scrum-half Conor Murray to work his magic.

In the backs, Johnny Sexton is a genius at leading Ireland around the field, Jacob Stockdale is the Irish 'find' of the decade and the experience and finishing skills of Rob Kearney and Keith Earls mean Ireland can cause chaos all over the pitch while also being impressively dedicated in defence.

However, where they do have questions to answer is how they cope going into big tournaments as one of the favourites.

They were expected to storm the 2019 Six Nations but an opening round loss to England, in Dublin no less, may suggest they prefer to stay under the radar when expectation and plaudits are being dished out.

What is clear is that they will be heavy favourites to top Pool A – although they will have to sweat to get there.

Scotland will be just as keen to open their campaign with a victory, Japan will be as fired up as any Rugby World Cup side ever as they seek to delight their home fans and both Russia and Samoa will be keen to prove their physical point.

One interesting issue for Ireland to control is the retirement of Schmidt, who will step down after RWC 2019.

Although pencilled in as a future All Blacks coach, Schmidt has opted to leave the game instead.

He will be as desperately keen as anyone to keep the spotlight on his players and their efforts on the pitch, rather than get drawn into a long farewell.

In one sense though, he more than deserves all the plaudits he is likely to receive from Ireland's fans thanks to the brilliant job he has done in charge of the national side, especially the beating of the All Blacks in 2016 – finally, at the 29th time of asking – and again in 2018 plus the Grand Slam that year.

For Schmidt, and Ireland, it has been a hugely exciting, invigorating and fruitful ride.

And Schmidt is hoping there is one last hurrah in the tanks of his charges.

SCOTLAND

FINN RUSSELL

When Finn Russell clicks then Scotland click. The playmaker loves the big stage and that is why many are backing the Racing 92 man to thrive in Japan. In the second half of the Six Nations match against England at Twickenham earlier this year he was the main reason why the visitors came back from 31-7 down to grab an amazing 38-38 draw. He always seems to have so much time on the ball and his eye for a gap and range of passing are second to none. He plays with an assured swagger and the fly-half from Stirling could well set Rugby World Cup 2019 alight.

COACH

GREGOR TOWNSEND

Having represented his country at two Rugby World Cups during an illustrious career in which he earned 82 Scotland caps and turned out for the British and Irish Lions, it was always likely that Gregor Townsend was going to coach the national team one day. He earned his stripes with Glasgow Warriors, helping them to PRO12 silverware in 2015, and took over Scotland in June 2017. The last two and a bit years under his stewardship have had some highs and some lows, but the way he has set his team up to play with adventure and flair has been welcomed by the Scottish rugby public.

IRELAND
SCOTLAND
JAPAN
RUSSIA
SAMOA

POOL A

SCOTLAND
RUGBY WORLD CUP STATISTICS

World Ranking	RWC Titles	RWC Apps
7	0	8

38 MATCHES PLAYED

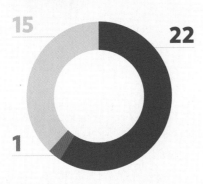

15
22
1

● Won ● Lost ● Drawn

Points scored:	Tries scored:
1,142	132
Average per match:	**Average per match:**
30.1	3.47

Conversions:	Penalties:	Drop goals:
97	104	10

Red cards:	Yellow cards:
0	5

POOL A FIXTURES

IRELAND
Sun 22 Sep, 16:45
International Stadium
Yokohama

SAMOA
Mon 30 Sep, 19:15
Kobe Misaki Stadium

RUSSIA
Wed 09 Oct, 16:15
Shizuoka Stadium
Ecopa

JAPAN
Sun 13 Oct, 19:45
International Stadium
Yokohama

OVERVIEW

Scotland came within a whisker of making the Rugby World Cup 2015 semi-finals, but were edged out by Australia in the last eight at Twickenham.

However, the expansive game that Scotland employed that day in London to nearly shock the Wallabies in the 35-34 loss left their supporters enthusiastic going forward.

They began 2016 with Six Nations victories over Italy and France and they then won two tough matches in Japan on their June tour.

In the November of that year they were again edged out by Australia by a point before defeating Argentina and Georgia.

The 2017 Six Nations saw Scotland on top form at home, defeating Ireland, Wales and Italy, with the latter game being the last in charge for Vern Cotter.

It was fitting that in the Kiwi's final match the Scots scored some good tries in a 29-0 victory at Murrayfield.

Gregor Townsend then came in and has continued to try and develop Scotland's squad and style of play.

In 2018 the highlights for the Scots included a 25-13 win over England to win the Calcutta Cup during the Six Nations and a 44-15 victory in June away to Argentina.

Low points included two away defeats to Wales and a 30-29 defeat in the USA. Heading into 2019, consistency was the thing that the team were really searching for.

The 2019 Six Nations perhaps did not go quite as they had hoped, but it certainly did not lack talking points. An opening win came against Italy ahead of losses to Ireland, France and Wales, before they were offered huge hope for RWC 2019 thanks to the way they performed against England.

In the final Six Nations match, they fought back for a 38-38 draw at Twickenham in one of the best ever rugby contests.

A number of young players have been making their mark of late, including back three players Darcy Graham and Blair Kinghorn, while back-row Jamie Ritchie is a great talent and Stuart McInally just gets better and better.

Scotland have played in all eight Rugby World Cups to date.

In 1987 they reached the last eight before losing to New Zealand, and then went one better by making the semi-finals in 1991. There they were beaten 9-6 by England and eventually finished fourth. Four years later they made it to the last eight before again being undone by New Zealand.

At Rugby World Cup 1999 a quarter-final berth was theirs again before, you guessed it, New Zealand got the better of them.

This century they have been quarter-finalists in 2003 and 2007 before failing to get out of their pool for the first time in 2011.

Four years ago they went close in the last eight against Australia, as mentioned.

This time around Scotland will be hopeful of making it to the knockout stages and then they know they can beat anyone on their day given some of the flair players they have in their ranks.

"We've got to be ready to play with energy, huge effort and be fitter than every team we come up against," Townsend said.

"That will enable us to attack and defend at a high level and put pressure on the opposition.

"There are a number of challenges that await us in the tournament, starting with facing some quality teams in our pool as well as adapting to Japan's unique environment."

JAPAN

MICHAEL LEITCH

Captain Michael Leitch makes Japan tick and leads by example from the back-row. He was born in New Zealand, but moved to Japan when he was 15 to study. He loved life there and in 2008 captained the under-20 side at the Junior World Championship. Soon after he would make his full debut against the USA and has been a regular in the squad over the last decade or so, progressing to lead the side. After he played in Rugby World Cup 2011 he was appointed Japan captain in April 2014, becoming the second New Zealand-born player to lead the Brave Blossoms after Andrew McCormick.

JAMIE JOSEPH

Jamie Joseph entered coaching after a playing career in which he not only won 20 caps for the All Blacks – but also made nine appearances for the RWC 2019 hosts. After retiring in 2001, Joseph returned to New Zealand, rising through the coaching ranks at Wellington Lions, as well as taking in spells with the Maori All Blacks. He made the step up to Super Rugby in 2011, guiding the Highlanders to their first ever title in 2015, before, in January 2016, announcing he was moving back to Japan to coach the Brave Blossoms, where he has beaten Italy, drawn with France and given Wales the fright of their lives.

IRELAND
SCOTLAND
JAPAN
RUSSIA
SAMOA

POOL A

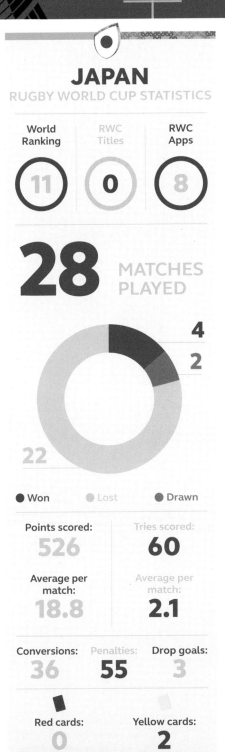

JAPAN
RUGBY WORLD CUP STATISTICS

World Ranking	RWC Titles	RWC Apps
11	0	8

28 MATCHES PLAYED

4
2
22

● Won　● Lost　● Drawn

Points scored:	Tries scored:
526	60

Average per match:	Average per match:
18.8	2.1

Conversions:	Penalties:	Drop goals:
36	55	3

Red cards:	Yellow cards:
0	2

POOL A FIXTURES

RUSSIA
Fri 20 Sep, 19:45
Tokyo Stadium

IRELAND
Sat 28 Sep, 16:15
Shizuoka Stadium
Ecopa

SAMOA
Sat 05 Oct, 19:30
City of Toyota
Stadium

SCOTLAND
Sun 13 Oct, 19:45
International Stadium
Yokohama

OVERVIEW

Japan were the talk of Rugby World Cup 2015 after their shock 34-32 victory over South Africa and with them hosting RWC 2019, rugby fever has once again hit the country.

In 2016, after the excitement of their big result in the showpiece event the previous year had died down, they got back to business and won their first four matches of the year against Korea and Hong Kong twice respectively.

That gave them confidence and they performed very well in a 26-22 victory over Canada before losing out to Scotland in two test matches, while pushing them hard.

A tough defeat against Argentina followed, but in November a 28-22 away win against Georgia in Tbilisi was the highlight.

As 2016 had started, 2017 began with two victories apiece against Korea and Hong Kong, before a good 33-21 triumph over Romania that June.

Ireland then travelled to Japan and emerged victorious from two tests, but they certainly knew they had been in a contest.

A big loss to Australia was next, but this team are nothing if not resilient, and a 39-6 triumph over Tonga in Toulouse set them up to give France a really big fright the following week.

In that November test in Paris, Japan were trailing at the break but fought back to draw 23-23 with Shota Horie, Timothy Lafaele and Asaeli Ai Valu scoring tries as they came close to toppling another of the world's top teams. That underlined their continuing development and the following year started with a tied series against Italy, Japan winning 34-17 in Oita with Italy then levelling things

up with a 25-22 triumph in Kobe.

A cracking 28-0 win over Georgia followed before two defeats in November against New Zealand and England. The team licked their wounds though and finished the year with a bang, seeing off Russia 32-27 in Gloucester in England, despite having been 22-10 down at the interval.

Captain Michael Leitch and fellow back-row Hendrik Tui scored tries in that one and both are key when it comes to getting Japan on the front foot.

Experienced Brave Blossoms performers like Horie, Masataka Mikami and Yu Tamura will also look to inspire their fellow countrymen – and the excited, partisan crowds – as Japan look to qualify for the quarter-finals for the first time.

Japan are proud to have been at every Rugby World Cup since 1987 and coach Jamie Joseph is excited about leading his side into the first ever tournament to be held in Asia.

"We will spend more time together, in fact we will spend the whole year together, and that is going to be needed if we are going to do well at the World Cup," he said.

"What I am seeing now is players who are confident, players that are proactive, players that are trying things in a game.

"They are not worried about making mistakes, not worried about failure but instead just excited about having a go.

"I think this is how they are going to win."

Pool A looks like a tough one to get out of with Ireland, Scotland, Samoa and Russia all just as desperate to progress, but Japan will be looking to build on their success at RWC 2015 – and since – to show they belong in the knockout stages.

RUSSIA

YURY KUSHNAREV
No-one has scored more test points or won more caps for Russia than the veteran fly-half. He made his international bow for the Bears back in November 2005 against the Czech Republic in Krasnodar, scoring a try, conversion and penalty, and has played test rugby in every calendar year since. Kushnarev made three appearances at RWC 2011 in New Zealand, while his 100th game for his country came against Namibia in November 2018. After missing out on RWC 2015, Russia will be looking forward to Kushnarev adding to his record haul of 756 international points.

LYN JONES
Appointed Russia coach in August 2018, the former openside won five caps for Wales in 1993. He began his coaching career the following year with Neath but forged his reputation with the Ospreys between 2003 and 2008, winning two Celtic League titles and the Anglo-Welsh Cup. Stints followed with London Welsh before he returned to Wales with the Dragons. He spent the 2017-18 season with Namibian side Welwitschias before taking the Bears job. Jones is known as something of a maverick in coaching circles and is the second Welshman after Kingsley Jones to take charge of the Russian national side.

IRELAND
SCOTLAND
JAPAN
RUSSIA
SAMOA

POOL A

RUSSIA
RUGBY WORLD CUP STATISTICS

World Ranking	RWC Titles	RWC Apps
20	0	1

4 MATCHES PLAYED

4

● Won   ● Lost   ● Drawn

Points scored:	Tries scored:
57	8

Average per match:	Average per match:
14.3	2

Conversions:	Penalties:	Drop goals:
4	2	1

Red cards:	Yellow cards:
0	0

POOL A FIXTURES

JAPAN
Fri 20 Sep, 19:45
Tokyo Stadium

SAMOA
Tue 24 Sep, 19:15
Kumagaya Rugby Stadium

IRELAND
Thu 03 Oct, 19:15
Kobe Misaki Stadium

SCOTLAND
Wed 09 Oct, 16:15
Shizuoka Stadium Ecopa

OVERVIEW

There's no trace of false modesty when Russia head coach Lyn Jones says his side "have a mountain to climb" at Rugby World Cup 2019. The Bears will be the third lowest ranked nation in Japan and, having appeared in only one previous tournament, Jones' team are short of pedigree and experience on rugby's biggest and most intimidating of stages.

Russia made their tournament bow at RWC 2011 in New Zealand. It proved a chastening experience as the Bears lost all four of their fixtures, conceding 196 points in the process, and Jones is acutely aware that any victory in Pool A this year would be a significant achievement.

In truth the Bears are lucky to have qualified for Japan at all. They finished outside the top two of the 2017 and 2018 Rugby Europe Championship but when an independent judicial and disputes committee imposed point penalties on runners-up Romania and third-placed Spain for fielding ineligible players, Russia were promoted to second. Whether they can make the most of their good fortune ramains to be seen.

They kick off their campaign against Japan in Tokyo in the tournament opener and although Russia can cite a victory against the Brave Blossoms in the same city back in 2003, few would confidently back the Bears to upset the hosts in front of a partisan 50,000-strong crowd in the capital.

The Pool A rivals, however, met as recently as November 2018 at Kingsholm in Gloucester, a match Japan narrowly edged 32-27.

The odds of ambushing the tier one powers of Ireland or Scotland are as long as Russia's border with Europe. The Irish comfotably beat Russia 62-12 in Rotorua at RWC 2011 and although Russia have never faced Scotland, Jones would have to conjure up something truly seismic to topple either one of the Six Nations pair.

Russia's best chance of opening their Rugby World Cup account will surely come against Samoa in Kumagaya in their second match.

The two countries have never crossed paths before and although the Pacific Islanders are the higher ranked of the two, the Bears will focus all their efforts on the fixture in the knowledge the match is essentially their 'final'.

Their form leading into RWC 2019 has been respectable if far from stellar. Victory in the 2017 Cup of Nations in Hong Kong – beating the hosts, Kenya and Chile – was undoubtedly a feather in the Russian cap but they were off the pace in the Rugby Europe Championship in 2019, finishing fourth after two wins from five.

By Jones' own admission, the Bears' greatest challenge in their second RWC appearance will be the squad's fitness levels, but it is an issue the Welshman and his coaching staff are desperate to address.

"In the Japan game [in November 2018] the ball was in play for 40 minutes which is 50 per cent more than these boys have done in their lives," he says.

"We have a plan to take us to the World Cup in the best possible condition that will allow us to compete and perform.

"There is no magic formula, just bloody hard work and organisation, and the Russian boys aren't afraid of hard work. They're moving in the right direction."

SAMOA

ED FIDOW

With a hulking frame of 1.88m and 97kgs, opponents who come up against 26-year-old Teofilo "Ed" Fidow at RWC 2019 may have wished they stayed at home. Fidow only made his test debut for Samoa in June last year but he quickly stamped himself as the team's most potent attacking weapon, scoring eight tries in his first seven tests, including a hat-trick against Germany in the RWC 2019 qualifiers. After developing his skills in the World Rugby Sevens Series, Fidow played for Brisbane City in Australia's NRC before being signed by Provence in France's D2. He will join Worcester Warriors for their 2019-20 campaign.

STEVE JACKSON

The man tasked with turning around the Pacific giants is former New Zealand Maori representative and Blues Super Rugby assistant coach, Steve Jackson. Auckland-born Jackson enjoyed a long and successful career as a player for Tasman, Auckland, North Harbour and Southland, where he was captain. In terms of coaching he was an assistant at Tasman and Counties Manukau before being handed his first head coach role at North Harbour, who he took to the Championship in New Zealand's second tier in 2016. But Jackson has his work cut out with Samoa who now find themselves at their lowest ever World Ranking of 16 just months out from RWC 2019.

IRELAND
SCOTLAND
JAPAN
RUSSIA
SAMOA

POOL **A**

SAMOA
RUGBY WORLD CUP STATISTICS

World Ranking	RWC Titles	RWC Apps
16	0	7

28 MATCHES PLAYED

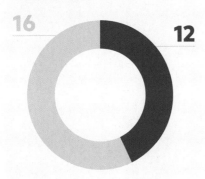

16

12

● Won   ● Lost   ● Drawn

Points scored:	Tries scored:
654	77

Average per match:	Average per match:
23.4	2.75

Conversions:	Penalties:	Drop goals:
49	61	2

Red cards:	Yellow cards:
2	6

POOL A FIXTURES

RUSSIA	SCOTLAND
Tue 24 Sep, 19:15 Kumagaya Rugby Stadium	Mon 30 Sep, 19:15 Kobe Misaki Stadium

JAPAN	IRELAND
Sat 5 Oct, 19:30 City of Toyota Stadium	Sat 12 Oct, 19:45 Fukuoka Hakatanomori Stadium

OVERVIEW

New coach Steve Jackson has an enormous task to take Manu Samoa back to the giddy heights of the 1990s when they reached the quarter-finals of both Rugby World Cup 1991 and 1995.

Back then, with legends like Frank Bunce, Brian Lima, Stephen Bachop, Apollo Perelini and Pat Lam leading the charge, Samoa achieved what is perhaps their greatest ever result – a 16-13 victory over Wales at Cardiff Arms Park in 1991.

Samoa's journey ended with defeat to Scotland at Murrayfield but they returned four years later, claiming the scalps of Argentina and Italy in the pool stages before being knocked out by the host nation South Africa, who were on their way to winning the tournament.

Since then Samoa have enjoyed some bright moments at Rugby World Cup – defeating Wales again in 1999 and Pacific rivals Fiji in 2011 and almost pulling off a famous victory over Scotland at England 2015 – but overall they have failed to live up to their undoubted potential.

The last four years have been an especially barren spell, with the once proud Pacific nation winning just five of their 20 test matches since RWC 2015, with their only successes in the last two years coming against emerging nations Germany and Spain.

Indeed, Samoa only guaranteed their participation at Japan 2019 with back-to-back victories over Germany in their Europe/Oceania play-off in June/July last year.

Samoa certainly boast some quality players in barnstorming Newcastle Falcons prop Logovi'i Mulipola, Bay of Plenty second-row Kane Le'aupepe and speedy winger Ed Fidow.

They also have the experience of 37-year-old fly-half Tusi Pisi, who will be playing in his third tournament, and strong leadership from flanker Jack Lam, cousin of Samoan legend Pat Lam.

Jackson is well aware of what is needed to make Samoa a force to be reckoned with and since his appointment, in October last year, he has made no secret of his aim to tempt players of Samoan heritage to pull on the famous blue jersey.

He says the coaching staff had a list of around 70 players eligible for Samoa that they were actively monitoring and he received messages from numerous players keen to play at Japan 2019.

"There's lots of speculation around other players but we're just focusing on the guys that we know that are available and eligible at the moment," Jackson said.

How successful Jackson is in this recruitment process will make a massive difference to Samoa's RWC 2019 performances.

Japan 2019 sees Samoa again with a tough task, finding themselves in the very competitive Pool A with 2018 Six Nations Grand Slam winners Ireland, Scotland, hosts Japan and Russia.

They lost to Scotland and Japan at England 2015 but will need to beat both in 2019 if they are to reach the quarter-finals for the first time after a gap of an astonishing 24 years – and fill Samoan hearts with pride as they did in Cardiff all those years ago.

EY
Building a better
working world

Does the final score
tell the whole story?

www.eyjapan.jp

The better the question.
The better the answer.
The better the world works.

POOL B

There can only be one favourite in any pool containing New Zealand, but if there was ever a time to fancy your chances against the current world champions, then this is it.

Despite currently topping the World Rugby Rankings, the All Blacks' aura of invincibility has shifted a little in the last 18 months, following defeat to Ireland and a narrow win over England in a less than convincing visit to the northern hemisphere in November, and a loss and a skin-of-their-teeth win against Pool B rivals South Africa in last year's Rugby Championship. That being said, there's a reason they remain top of most pundits' lists to not only top Pool B but win the tournament as a whole and while some may see vulnerabilities, those losses could simply act as motivation to win it all again this year.

New Zealand's Rugby World Cup 2019 opener provides the marquee fixture for Pool B, coming as it does against their major rivals South Africa, with the losers likely facing Ireland, rather than Scotland or Japan, in the quarter-finals.

Semi-finalists in 2015, the Springboks have been rebuilding nicely under coach Rassie Erasmus, who has managed to pull together one of the most harmonious squads in years. Despite losing more matches in 2018 than 2017, and scoring fewer tries, statistics can be deceiving, and the aforementioned win over New Zealand (their first over the All Blacks since 2009), a home series victory against England and wins over France and Scotland in November

will give them belief they can go far in Japan. When they decide to switch on, they can match any team in the world.

It's tough to see past those two tournament heavyweights to find anyone else who could trouble the knockout stages of RWC 2019.

Italy beat South Africa in November 2016 but swiftly lost to Tonga a week later, and since then it has been the usual tale of Six Nations woes and defeats to other tier one teams (as well as Japan in June last year), and unconvincing wins over the likes of Georgia and Fiji.

It would take a spectacular upset to see the Azzurri make it out of the pool for the first time, and that applies even more so to Namibia and Canada.

Namibia will have a vulnerable Italy in their sights, though, having made steady improvement over the last few years. No longer a team that concedes cricket scores, they reached their sixth successive Rugby World Cup by winning the Africa qualifiers, and despite never winning at the tournament, they produced a spirited performance against the All Blacks in 2015, before losing to Georgia by just one point.

Canada were the final team to qualify after winning the repechage. Coached by ex-Gloucester and Sale star Kingsley Jones, and former England centre Henry Paul, their success will largely be measured by their result against Namibia.

NEW ZEALAND

RIEKO IOANE

Such is the abundance of talent at New Zealand's disposal that their entire squad could easily grab this title. But one who edges most is prodigious try-scoring winger Rieko Ioane. The All Blacks are the most exciting attacking team on the planet and the man more often than not finishing off those deadly attacks is Ioane, who notched up 22 tries in his first 24 tests, and is already well on track to breaking Doug Howlett's impressive All Blacks record of 49 test tries. If the powerful Rio 2016 Olympian gets into space very few will catch him.

COACH

STEVE HANSEN

All Blacks coach Steve Hansen will be looking for the perfect send-off having already announced that he will step down after RWC 2019. A former Wales coach from 2002-04, Hansen can lay claim to being one of the most successful national coaches of all time since taking over from Graham Henry after RWC 2011. Under his watch the All Blacks became the first nation to ever retain the Webb Ellis Cup in England four years ago and are favourites to do the same in Japan. His winning ratio hovers around 90 per cent and he has won six of the seven Rugby Championships he has contested.

NEW ZEALAND
SOUTH AFRICA
ITALY
NAMIBIA
CANADA

POOL B

NEW ZEALAND
RUGBY WORLD CUP STATISTICS

World Ranking	RWC Titles	RWC Apps
1	**3**	**8**

50 MATCHES PLAYED

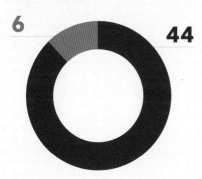

6   44

● Won   ● Lost   ● Drawn

Points scored:	Tries scored:
2,302	**311**
Average per match:	Average per match:
46.04	**6.22**

Conversions:	Penalties:	Drop goals:
228	**109**	**10**

Red cards:	Yellow cards:
0	**9**

POOL B FIXTURES

SOUTH AFRICA
Sat 21 Sep, 18:45
International Stadium Yokohama

CANADA
Wed 02 Oct, 19:15
Oita Stadium

NAMIBIA
Sun 06 Oct, 13:45
Tokyo Stadium

ITALY
Sat 12 Oct, 13:45
City of Toyota Stadium

OVERVIEW

Widely regarded as one of the most successful teams in any sport on the planet, the All Blacks are synonymous with excellence and setting the benchmark for how well the game can be played. Not only do New Zealand win but they do it in a style that is fast, highly skilled and often breathtaking.

The All Blacks raised the Webb Ellis Cup in the very first Rugby World Cup in New Zealand in 1987, as they did again in 2011 and for a third time in England in 2015. Very few would bet against them doing so again in 2019.

To give some idea of how New Zealand have dominated men's 15s over the last decade, they reclaimed the World Rugby Rankings No.1 spot from South Africa in late 2009 and have held it ever since.

In that time they have won two Rugby World Cups, seven Rugby Championships and 11 straight Bledisloe Cups. Indeed six of the last seven winners of the World Rugby Player of the Year have hailed from New Zealand with only Ireland's Johnny Sexton managing to break the sequence last year.

So impressive is the All Blacks' winning record that 2018, when they lost two tests out of 14 (one in Wellington against the Springboks and another in Dublin against Ireland), was perceived as a poor year and speculation mounted that their crown was slipping.

Nothing could be further from the truth. Since RWC 2015 they may have lost legends such as Richie McCaw and Dan Carter, two of the greatest to ever play the game, but new greats, such as captain Kieran Read and fly-half Beauden Barrett, have simply stepped up to take their places.

Due to their superb development pathways and excellent player retention the All Blacks have a deep talent pool that is the envy of the rest of the world. In every position they have not one or two, but often three players who would be close to the best in the world.

Players like utility back Damian McKenzie, fly-half Richie Mo'unga and blockbusting centre Ngani Laumape would be guaranteed starting roles for any other nation on earth but they must bide their time for the All Blacks, making the most of the few opportunities that come their way.

This phenomenal depth also keeps opponents guessing as the All Blacks can mix and match their line-up and replacements so they are almost impossible to stop. The credit for this, of course, goes to head coach Steve Hansen, but also CEO Steve Tew, who has done a superb job guiding New Zealand Rugby since the disappointment of RWC 2007.

In terms of playing style the All Blacks simply have no weaknesses. As Hansen will continually re-affirm, although they have the most dynamic backline on the planet, nothing can be achieved without winning the battle upfront and in second-rows Sam Whitelock and Brodie Retallick, props Owen Franks and Joe Moody, and either Dane Coles or Codie Taylor at hooker, New Zealand can mix it with anyone.

If they have any chink at all it is perhaps in the back row where injuries to Sam Cane, Read and Liam Squire have been disruptive, but with stars like Shannon Frizell and Ardie Savea ready to step in – it is a gap that is quickly closed.

New Zealand are understandably a very proud rugby nation and with a clever coach, settled squad and many of the best players on the globe they will be more than disappointed not to extend their record and claim a fourth Rugby World Cup in Japan.

SOUTH AFRICA

SPRINGBOKS

STAR MAN

MALCOLM MARX

A nominee for World Rugby Player of the Year in 2018, Marx is the man-mountain the Springboks have been looking for. Physically imposing and tough at the breakdown, Marx has risen through the junior ranks to lay claim to possibly being the world's best hooker at the moment. His physicality, uncompromising attitude and ability to steal ball around the field has made him an exceptional asset for the Springboks, and a player that opposition teams fear. An expert jackal on his own tryline, more than one team has cursed his prowess in robbing them of their ball.

COACH

RASSIE ERASMUS

When he was appointed, Erasmus was hailed in some quarters as the saviour of South Africa. After the tenure of Allister Coetzee, Springboks fans were looking for a new dawn, and Erasmus gave it to them. He started off with a series win over England, but has had mixed results in the test arena. Erasmus is a pragmatic coach, a believer in systems and has been working tirelessly in trying to get them in place before the tournament. A firm believer in playing an attacking brand of rugby, Erasmus will try and build a solid foundation up front, while giving his team the tools out wide to score tries.

NEW ZEALAND
SOUTH AFRICA
ITALY
NAMIBIA
CANADA

POOL B

SOUTH AFRICA
RUGBY WORLD CUP STATISTICS

World Ranking	RWC Titles	RWC Apps
5	2	6

36 MATCHES PLAYED

6   30

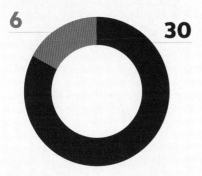

● Won   ● Lost   ● Drawn

Points scored:	Tries scored:
1,250	141
Average per match:	Average per match:
34.7	3.9

Conversions:	Penalties:	Drop goals:
103	98	15

Red cards:	Yellow cards:
2	8

POOL B FIXTURES

 NEW ZEALAND
Sat 21 Sep, 18:45
International Stadium Yokohama

 NAMIBIA
Sat 28 Sep, 18:45
City of Toyota Stadium

 ITALY
Fri 04 Oct, 18:45
Shizuoka Stadium Ecopa

 CANADA
Tue 08 Oct, 19:15
Kobe Misaki Stadium

OVERVIEW

It is understandable that South Africa's own fans may not give them too much of a chance for this year's Rugby World Cup.

After a rollercoaster four years where they plumbed the depths in terms of results, and suffered a massive player exodus and internal challenges that saw them drop out of the top four in the World Rugby Rankings, few would make them serious contenders for the Webb Ellis Cup.

But that would be a short-sighted, poor assessment of the current state of Springboks rugby.

Under coach Rassie Erasmus, several steps have been taken over the past year to increase depth and get the national team back to their former glory, taking into consideration the challenges that a growing rugby population plying their trade in Europe and Japan has on the national side.

The Springboks have shown in the past – most notably in 1995 and 2007 where they lifted the trophy – that they are a side that can turn it on when it is needed. Semi-finalists at RWC 1999 and 2015, they have the ability to put together performances that could beat any team in the competition, losing only to New Zealand 20-18 at Twickenham last time out.

But while this is true, their consistency over the past few years has given their opponents confidence as well.

This is no longer the physical colossus that teams try to avoid as they have in the past, and Japan's magnificent victory in Brighton four years ago has left a scar on the psyche.

Erasmus has taken the side and built it slowly, not always getting the results, but

always with this tournament in mind. In Siya Kolisi he has a leader that is an inspiration to the South African nation and dons the No.6 jersey worn by Francois Pienaar and Nelson Mandela in 1995.

The Springboks have reverted to their traditional game plan of solid set-pieces and a towering lineout – and this is where Pieter-Steph du Toit, Malcolm Marx and Eben Etzebeth are the key members of their forward juggernaut.

But at the back they have added the exuberance of Faf de Klerk – a nominee for World Rugby Player of the Year with Marx last year – and have a confident Willie le Roux marshalling from the back.

And they have speed aplenty. World Rugby Breakthrough Player of the Year Aphiwe Dyantyi is part of a new breed of Springbok, with his wing partner S'bu Nkosi no stranger to the tryline.

These Springboks may be hard to predict, but they can certainly scare many of the main contenders for the title, and they have no fear of the All Blacks either. Their epic win in Wellington last year was the first time New Zealand lost at home in decades and was the elixir that Erasmus needed a year out from this competition.

To Springboks fans, South Africa will always be expected to win the tournament, no matter what.

They may not be among the favourites or the teams that many talk about ahead of RWC 2019, but Erasmus has been building slowly, surely towards the tournament.

And he knows if the pieces fall into place according to his plans, South Africa will be contenders. No matter what their recent results say.

ITALY

STAR MAN

SERGIO PARISSE

The word legend is overused these days in sport, but there is no doubt in any rugby fan's mind that Sergio Parisse is a true legend. Rugby World Cup 2019 will be the fifth showpiece event that the talismanic captain and number eight will have been involved in, having also played in 2003, 2007, 2011 and 2015. He has been in and around the Italy set-up for an amazing 17 years and even when he was a young player making his way in the game he did not look out of place at the top level. If he plays well then Italy play well, it is as simple as that. A true icon and talisman, he deserves a great tournament.

COACH

CONOR O'SHEA

It is always good to have a head coach who has been to showpiece events before and for Italy, Conor O'Shea ticks that box. He was a full-back for Ireland during his playing days, earning 35 caps and playing at RWC 1995 and 1999. Fast forward a few years and, after a career-ending injury, he got into coaching at London Irish in 2001. He had stints with the Rugby Football Union and Harlequins before his opportunity in international coaching arrived with Italy in 2016. There have been some tough results since he took up the post, but it feels like O'Shea is taking Italian rugby in the right direction.

NEW ZEALAND
SOUTH AFRICA
ITALY
NAMIBIA
CANADA

POOL B

ITALY
RUGBY WORLD CUP STATISTICS

World Ranking	RWC Titles	RWC Apps
14	0	8

28 MATCHES PLAYED

17   11

● Won   ● Lost   ● Drawn

Points scored:	Tries scored:
529	**54**
Average per match:	Average per match:
18.9	1.9

Conversions:	Penalties:	Drop goals:
38	**62**	**3**

Red cards:	Yellow cards:
0	6

POOL B FIXTURES

NAMIBIA	CANADA
Sun 22 Sep, 14:15	Thu 26 Sep, 16:45
Hanazono Rugby Stadium	Fukuoka Hakatanomori Stadium

SOUTH AFRICA	NEW ZEALAND
Fri 04 Oct, 18:45	Sat 12 Oct, 13:45
Shizuoka Stadium Ecopa	City of Toyota Stadium

OVERVIEW

After a poor performance in the Six Nations of 2016, Conor O'Shea took up the post of Italy head coach in June of that year, but lost his first match 30-24 in Argentina.

Wins in the USA and Canada showed the new man that he had the basis of a good squad to work with though, and he wanted to build from there.

Yet it is Italy's inconsistency that continues to frustrate their fans and has seen O'Shea come in for criticism in the build up to Japan.

Their preparation for this tournament has not been ideal as a winless Six Nations in 2018 was repeated earlier this year.

Like in 2018, they played their best rugby in the final game against France, but despite creating a lot of chances they eventually ran out of steam and lost 25-14.

And certainly that means that attacking accuracy is something they will want to improve on at Rugby World Cup 2019.

Italy have never made it out of the pool stages at the showpiece event.

At Rugby World Cup 1987 they bounced back from defeats to New Zealand and Argentina to score a famous victory over Fiji.

In 1991 they managed a cracking 30-9 win over the USA and they pushed New Zealand pretty hard before losing out to them 31-21.

Again, in 1995, they pushed a big team close before going down to England 27-20.

In 1999 they lost all of their matches before bouncing back in 2003, recording two wins at the event for the first time.

Those came against Tonga and Canada, but they still finished third in the pool behind New Zealand and Wales.

In 2007 they defeated Portugal and Romania, but were edged out into second place in the pool by Scotland, who just hung on to see them off 18-16.

Two wins came in 2011 and 2015, but they were edged out of possible knockout stage qualification by Ireland and Australia, and Ireland and France.

All in all then, Rugby World Cups have been relatively forgettable events for Italy – and they face an extremely difficult task this time as well.

Pool B is expected to be dominated by New Zealand and South Africa while both Namibia and Canada have improved in recent times.

Italy will be hoping to beat those two nations, but nothing is guaranteed. However, in their favour is a dedicated, tight unit with players such as scrum-half Tito Tebaldi and veteran forwards Leonardo Ghiraldini and Alessandro Zanni desperate to impress.

Sergio Parisse will feature in his fifth Rugby World Cup, the second Italian to achieve that feat after former team-mate Mauro Bergamasco managed it at RWC 2015.

Parisse and O'Shea have become incredibly close since the Irishman became Italy's head coach and he will be sorely missed when he moves on from the international stage.

O'Shea, though, believes Italy can – and must – improve in the coming years and he is dedicated to making that happen.

"To get to the highest level is always hard work and we have put in place things that were needed, but there is still loads to do," O'Shea said. "We are getting more competitive at test level and we will only get stronger."

NAMIBIA

RENALDO BOTHMA

Namibia has a solid reputation of producing international quality forwards such as Kees Lensing and Jacques Burger, to name just two. But Bothma is a classic physical barnstorming number eight who never takes a step back for anyone. Blessed with impressive stamina, good game-management and the ability to launch attacks from the back of the scrum, Bothma is a huge asset to his side. After stints for the Sharks and Bulls in Super Rugby, his move to Harlequins in England has been set back by injuries, but fit and raring to go again, Bothma will lead from the front and hope his team-mates will follow.

PHIL DAVIES

Welshman Phil Davies' profile suits the hardened Namibians down to a tee. As a former second-row for both Llanelli and Wales who was capped 46 times by his country, his no-nonsense approach to coaching and professionalism has gone down well in the African country. As head coach of Namibia since 2015, he has steered their qualification process and led them to second place in the World Rugby Nations Cup in 2016. Davies has also taken them to four consecutive Rugby Africa Gold Cup titles, proof indeed that Namibia are developing into a truly impressive outfit.

NEW ZEALAND
SOUTH AFRICA
ITALY
NAMIBIA
CANADA

POOL B

NAMIBIA
RUGBY WORLD CUP STATISTICS

World Ranking	RWC Titles	RWC Apps
23	**0**	**5**

19 MATCHES PLAYED

19

- ● Won
- ● Lost
- ● Drawn

Points scored:	Tries scored:
214	**24**
Average per match:	Average per match:
11.3	**1.3**

Conversions:	Penalties:	Drop goals:
17	**16**	**4**

Red cards:	Yellow cards:
1	**9**

POOL B FIXTURES

ITALY
Sun 22 Sep, 14:15
Hanazono Rugby Stadium

SOUTH AFRICA
Sat 28 Sep, 18:45
City of Toyota Stadium

NEW ZEALAND
Sun 06 Oct, 13:45
Tokyo Stadium

CANADA
Sun 13 Oct, 12:15
Kamaishi Recovery Memorial Stadium

OVERVIEW

Given their tournament history and their place in the World Rugby Rankings, Namibia head into RWC 2019 very much as underdogs, but they will be hoping to feed off this status to cause one or two surprises in Pool B.

It is a fact that Namibia have the worst Rugby World Cup record of all – losing all 19 matches they have appeared in at the showpiece tournament, and, being pooled with rugby giants New Zealand and South Africa, they face a huge task if they are to reverse their fortunes at Japan 2019.

However, there is still some hope that the African nation will harbour ambitions of their own, especially when facing Canada and Italy.

Possibly the biggest obstacle for Namibia is the lack of consistent opposition, and while they have been given a place in South Africa's domestic competitions, their Rugby Africa Gold Cup campaigns showed that if they are given an extended run as a squad, they can be more than competitive and build momentum to start becoming a force in International rugby.

After beating Kenya 53-28 at the Hage Geingob National Rugby Stadium last August to qualify for RWC 2019, Davies summed up the journey he and his charges are on. "We've got a good young squad," he said. "The squad is deeper than it's ever been, so let's hope we can develop the potential we have and make the country proud at the World Cup."

Namibia will certainly be proud – both on and off the pitch, and while they do not possess many big names bar Harlequins' superb number eight Renaldo Bothma, they will lack little in terms of fighting spirit and passion.

Full-back Chrysander Botha and centres Chad Plato and JC Greyling are all solid performers and capable of hurting teams, while a pack containing the likes of Casper Viviers, Obert Nortje, AJ de Klerk and Rohan Kitshoff will also ensure that opposition teams have to win the battle up front before they get the opportunity to score.

At RWC 2019, those performers will look to stave off big defeats against the All Blacks and Springboks, with the latter providing them a lot of motivation given the geographical borders between the two countries, and it will be against Italy and Canada that Namibia will measure their progress.

Considering that in 11 of Namibia's 19 defeats in Rugby World Cup history, the opposition has crossed the half-century mark, Davies and his squad will be looking to show measured improvement, be more difficult to beat in the set-piece and hold their own in defence.

A good showing will help spur on the development programme back home and show they do belong on the world stage, and it will show World Rugby's investment in the country has been put to good use.

The draw may be against the Namibians, and their hopes may be slim. But Davies has instilled a fighting spirit in the side that saw them overcome their African rivals to qualify for the tournament.

Now Davies will be hoping that complacency from their more-fancied rivals will give them an opening to show they can mix it with the bigger sides and surprise the rest of the world at the same time.

CANADA

STAR MAN

LUCAS RUMBALL

The pride of James Bay, British Columbia, Rumball epitomises the kind of play Canada needs at Rugby World Cup 2019. He doesn't back down, puts in more than a full day at the office, and embraces physicality. His unflinching approach has earned him a captain's nod during 2019, and the wild-haired flanker provides the full spectrum of skills, whether making key carries, winning ball, or always, always, making tackles. Rumball sees potential in the last few months. "Some results haven't gone our way but the boys have got stuck in there. We have a lot of positives to build on."

COACH

KINGSLEY JONES

Kingsley Jones took over as head coach of Canada when the team was at a low point, having just lost the Rugby World Cup qualifier series to USA. With an unsettled side and then a qualifier series loss to Uruguay, Jones was under pressure to get it right in the repechage. It was a difficult task, but Jones, who was part of the coaching team with Russia at RWC 2011, has embraced difficult tasks. He has smiled at player availability issues and called it a chance to test new talent. The repechage, he said, was a chance to put all the pieces together. It's that positivity that Canada will lean on going forward.

NEW ZEALAND
SOUTH AFRICA
ITALY
NAMIBIA
CANADA

CANADA
RUGBY WORLD CUP STATISTICS

World Ranking	RWC Titles	RWC Apps
21	**0**	**8**

29 MATCHES PLAYED

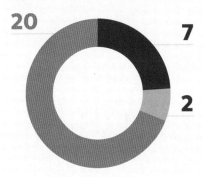

20

7

2

● Won   ◐ Lost   ◐ Drawn

Points scored:	Tries scored:
527	**56**

Average per match:	Average per match:
18.2	**1.9**

Conversions:	Penalties:	Drop goals:
33	**57**	**8**

Red cards:	Yellow cards:
3	**5**

POOL B FIXTURES

ITALY
Thu 26 Sep, 16:45
Fukuoka Hakatanomori
Stadium

NEW ZEALAND
Wed 02 Oct, 19:15
Oita Stadium

SOUTH AFRICA
Tue 08 Oct, 19:15
Kobe Misaki
Stadium

NAMIBIA
Sun 13 Oct, 12:15
Kamaishi Recovery
Memorial Stadium

OVERVIEW

Despite losing all four matches at Rugby World Cup 2015, Canada had reason to feel optimistic.

Two of those losses were achingly close – 17-15 to Romania and, even more notable, 23-18 to Italy.

But the results didn't flow as expected over the next four years. Nations that Canada expected to beat more often than not, such as Japan, Georgia, Uruguay, and, most difficult to take, the USA, were now elusive.

Winning three and losing two in the 2016 Americas Rugby Championship actually proved to be the post-2015 highlight as they failed to close out tight games.

After losing six games by less than a try in 2016 and 2017, the Canadians managed to pull off a draw against their rivals to the south in the first of a two-game Rugby World Cup qualifier. The return leg in San Diego, marred by the absence of try-scoring sensation DTH van der Merwe, was a huge disappointment, as the Eagles ran rampant to win 52-16. That loss cost head coach Mark Anscombe his job.

Since then, the team has seen significant player turnover, losing long-time captain Aaron Carpenter to retirement, due to repeated concussions, and superb back Conor Trainor to a ruptured Achilles.

Some of their overseas-based professionals may not have been available for every match, but the commitment to the Canadian cause has never been in doubt.

Rugby Canada merged the sevens and 15s programmes in 2018 to bolster preparations for the repechage, the team coming together for the final qualification chance in Marseille.

With major stars on the field, Canada blossomed.

Long-striding number eight Tyler Ardron was a force, second-row Brett Beukeboom dominated the point of contact, and backs Theo Sauder and Van der Merwe were exceptional out wide. Wins over Kenya, Hong Kong and Germany secured a spot at Japan 2019. Van der Merwe scored five tries in the three games.

At the centre of that rebound was Phil Mack. The 33-year-old scrum-half and member of the Toquaht Nation, one of Canada's indigenous peoples, captained his country through that tumultuous time. His role as a rescuer wasn't new; in 2018 Mack signed with the Seattle Seawolves of the new Major League Rugby (MLR) competition. Soon after, Seattle lost its coach, and Mack stepped in, not only to lead the team, but lead it to the championship.

Now looking towards RWC 2019, the Canadian team will put aside a string of disappointing results as head coach Kingsley Jones will finally have all of his healthy players available. That's a group that has benefitted greatly from the development of MLR – with one or two exceptions, the entire Canadian RWC 2019 squad will be professional.

And that team has a very clear goal: win two matches. Namibia are certainly on Canada's radar as a game to win, and Italy, while strong, have often had trouble with the Canucks.

Certainly New Zealand and South Africa know from their tournament experience that you come away from a test match against Canada knowing you have been pushed to the limits.

RUGBY
WORLD CUP™
JAPAN日本2019
SOFT DRINK SUPPLIER

SUNTORY
RWC 2019 SOFT DRINK SUPPLIER

Suntory supports Rugby World Cup 2019™ Japan!

Suntory natural mineral Water
is RWC 2019's Official Water.

GREEN DA·KA·RA
is RWC 2019's Official Isotonic.

The official soft drink of the tournament

POOL C

England Rugby

FRANCE RUGBY

USA RUGBY

TONGA

It seems every tournament has one and on the surface, this should be it: The Pool of Death. Given the form of the teams involved, however, that ominous tag could start to look a little misplaced.

England began 2018 ranked second in the world – after a two-year period in which they lost only to Ireland – with Argentina eighth and France ninth. But, fast forward to now, and although France have moved up a place to eighth, England have slipped to fourth and Argentina to 10th. With USA and Tonga making up the rest of the pool, it all feels slightly different to the 2015 version, which featured two Rugby World Cup winners (England and Australia), a flying Wales, and the physical Fiji and Uruguay.

What this pool is, though, is a pool of uncertainty. England will be favourites to finish top, but they, France and Argentina all have the potential to whitewash the pool, win all their matches and trot comfortably and confidently into the quarter-finals. However, experience tells us they also have the capability to fluff their lines, implode and leave the competition at the pool stage to return home, tails between their legs.

Eddie Jones will be hoping that, if nothing else, his four years in charge have instilled the mental toughness required for that not to happen to England, although their second half disintegration to Scotland, as well as defeat in Cardiff, in this year's Six Nations will have let a few nagging doubts come creeping back in. But they only need to look to their defeat of Ireland at the start of that tournament and a November international series in which they won three, and ran the All Blacks close, for inspiration ahead of RWC 2019.

France, like England, had a somewhat topsy-turvy 2018, but it is their enduring inconsistency which helps makes this pool such an intriguing one. They have shown some signs of improvement under Jacques Brunel, scoring a notable win over England in the 2018 Six Nations, but they suffered at the hands of New Zealand in June last year and lost to Fiji in November, before a disappointing Six Nations campaign at the start of this year.

And then there is Argentina, who, like France, have a history of stepping up a level at Rugby World Cups. Another team which hasn't been in great form (they won just twice in 2018), with the legendary Mario Ledesma at the helm they will be eyeing their encounter with England on 5 October as their shot at causing an upset. They will also fancy their chances against France on 21 September in Tokyo which, if England find their best form, could be the decisive match of the pool.

Tonga always seem to be a troublesome team come Rugby World Cup, as France know from their defeat in the 2011 pool stage, but their lack of exposure to the leading teams could be a telling factor. The USA, improving under coach Gary Gold, will hope to spring a surprise after a successful year in 2018, which included a first win over Scotland.

ENGLAND

STAR MAN

OWEN FARRELL

With his effective kicking, solid defence and ability to spot the tiniest of gaps in the opposition's defence, Owen Farrell is very much the archetypal modern-day fly-half. He spent the formative years of his international career switching between No.10 and inside-centre as England tried to find the best way of accommodating his skills, but he has become increasingly settled and effective at fly-half. He is at the heart of England's play whether going forward or in defence and his consistency helped see him nominated as World Rugby Player of the Year in 2012, 2016 and 2017.

COACH

EDDIE JONES

Jones' reputation as a world-class coach was already firmly cemented before he took over from Stuart Lancaster following England's RWC 2015 campaign and his time at Twickenham has re-affirmed his standing as one of the world's best, winning the Six Nations Grand Slam at the first time of asking in 2016. England are the third international side Jones has coached following spells with Australia and Japan. He was also South Africa's technical advisor when they won RWC 2007. Jones presents a stern face to the world's media but he undoubtedly knows how to get the best out of his squad, as England are proving.

ENGLAND
FRANCE
ARGENTINA
USA
TONGA

POOL C

ENGLAND
RUGBY WORLD CUP STATISTICS

World Ranking	RWC Titles	RWC Apps
4	**1**	**8**

44 MATCHES PLAYED

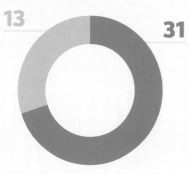

13

31

● Won   ● Lost   ● Drawn

Points scored:	Tries scored:
1,379	**147**
Average per match:	Average per match:
31.3	**3.3**

Conversions:	Penalties:	Drop goals:
107	**131**	**21**

Red cards:	Yellow cards:
0	**5**

POOL C FIXTURES

TONGA
Sun 22 Sep, 19:15
Sapporo Dome

USA
Thu 26 Sep, 19:45
Kobe Misaki Stadium

ARGENTINA
Sat 05 Oct, 17:00
Tokyo Stadium

FRANCE
Sat 12 Oct, 17:15
International Stadium Yokohama

OVERVIEW

It has certainly been a period to remember for England's fans since they last featured in a Rugby World Cup encounter.

Back at RWC 2015, England became the first host nation to go out at the pool stage after a disappointing tournament under Stuart Lancaster.

Yet their last Pool A match saw them beat Uruguay 60-3 and that was the start of an 18-match winning streak that only ended 18 months later in Dublin as Ireland prevented England from winning back-to-back Six Nations Grand Slams.

The transformation in fortunes, and England's ongoing development as a team, are a result of Eddie Jones' involvement as head coach.

He has forged a new togetherness in the camp and that fact, aligned with England's superb fitness and huge pool of players to choose from due to the success of the domestic game, ensures they will arrive at RWC 2019 in hopeful fashion.

However, not even the most optimistic England fan would suggest they are the finished article quite yet.

One of Jones' biggest tasks this year has been identifying why England can sometimes lack the consistency and killer-instinct required to win matches that they dominate.

That issue was demonstrated perfectly during the Six Nations as England squandered a healthy lead in a loss to Wales and then stood shellshocked as Scotland overturned a 31-0 deficit to take a 38-31 lead, before they desperately earned a 38-38 draw with the last kick of the match.

"The hardest lessons are the best lessons and you want them before the World Cup," Jones said. "You do that against Tonga in the pool stages of the World Cup for example and then you find yourselves in a difficult situation going forward.

"It's a great lesson for us, I'd rather have these problems now than at the World Cup. We know what the problem is but it's not easy to fix."

Jones may have concerns about how he is going to fix his 'problems' but many coaches in world rugby would love to have the selection headache the former Japan coach has.

Simply put, he has a plethora of genuinely world-class stars at his disposal and a team that has now played together for a considerable amount of time, creating the types of bonds that can make all the difference in tight situations.

In Owen Farrell and George Ford, England have two fine kickers and men who can open up even the tightest of defences, Jonny May is one of the fastest and most devastating finishers in world rugby, Manu Tuilagi's long-standing injury complaints appear to be behind him, and Joe Cokanasiga looks to be the real deal.

Meanwhile, a huge and mobile pack including players like Tom Curry, Billy Vunipola, Jamie George, Kyle Sinckler, Joe Launchbury and George Kruis all ensure that the traditionally English strengths of scrummaging and forward play remain as important to their style of play as ever.

Jones has made it clear that he does not think England are fulfilling their potential. Not quite yet. But what better time – and what better place – to change that than RWC 2019?

FRANCE

STAR MAN

GUILHEM GUIRADO

Given that historically France like to play with flair you might think that a back would be their key man, but given the leadership qualities of Guilhem Guirado, he is the obvious choice. The hooker has been around the national team set-up for some 11 years now and throughout all of the ups and downs he has been one of the constants. He never lets his performance level dip and is good with ball in hand, being used by head coach Jacques Brunel to carry often. The front-row man has previous experience of playing on this stage having been involved at both RWC 2011 and 2015.

COACH

JACQUES BRUNEL

Jacques Brunel has been in charge for nearly two years now and it is fair to say that his time at the top has been up and down. He is a very experienced coach having moved into that sphere over 30 years ago when his playing days ended in 1988. Brunel made his name at Auch then Colomiers before moving to Pau in 1999. From 2001 he was a member of the French national coaching set-up and went with the team to Rugby World Cup 2003 and 2007. Four years with Perpignan followed before five years with Italy and then this chance to lead his own national team was too good to turn down.

ENGLAND
FRANCE
ARGENTINA
USA
TONGA

POOL C

FRANCE
RUGBY WORLD CUP STATISTICS

World Ranking	RWC Titles	RWC Apps
8	0	8

48 MATCHES PLAYED

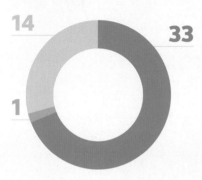

14
33
1

● Won ● Lost ● Drawn

Points scored:	Tries scored:
1,487	**172**

Average per match:	Average per match:
31	3.6

Conversions:	Penalties:	Drop goals:
122	**135**	**10**

Red cards:	Yellow cards:
0	9

POOL C FIXTURES

ARGENTINA
Sat 21 Sep, 16:15
Tokyo Stadium

USA
Wed 02 Oct, 16:45
Fukuoka Hakatanomori Stadium

TONGA
Sun 06 Oct, 16:45
Kumamoto Stadium

ENGLAND
Sat 12 Oct, 17:15
International Stadium Yokohama

OVERVIEW

The more France change, the more they stay the same.

There is no team in world rugby that is such a byword for 'inconsistent'. On their day, France remain one of the world's most watchable and exciting teams.

Yet they can disappoint as much as they can dazzle.

Their build-up to Rugby World Cup 2019 is another classic case of France flattering to deceive.

When you place their squad up against any other side going into RWC 2019 then it is crystal clear that France have talent in abundance.

Damian Penaud, Antoine Dupont, Romain Ntamack, Yoann Huget; this list of tough and tenacious players goes on and on.

Yet, the three-time Rugby World Cup finalists have not enjoyed the last few years as their long-held inability to find a settled and stable squad – and playing style – comes back to haunt them.

After RWC 2015, coach Guy Novés held on to his position until Jacques Brunel was brought in to steady the creaking ship in 2017.

In the new man's first game in charge in early 2018, the side went toe-to-toe with Ireland in the Six Nations before losing out to an injury-time drop goal.

A second loss came against Scotland in Edinburgh before Brunel got the first win of his tenure when France saw off Italy, his former charges, 34-17.

That seemed to give the team confidence because then came a landmark win over England with the forward pack and the little magician Maxime Machenaud on fire to turn a 9-9 half-time score into a 22-16 triumph.

The Six Nations ended with a tight loss in Wales before three heavy June losses in New Zealand.

A win did then come against Argentina the following November, but it was bookended by losses to South Africa and Fiji, the latter result really hurting Brunel as his tenure continued to be full of ups and downs.

The Six Nations earlier this year saw wins over Scotland and Italy, but they papered over the cracks a bit as Brunel still tinkered with things trying to find his best match-day 23.

And it is that issue that is such a problem for France, as a settled matchday squad is surely the number one priority of every coach going into RWC 2019, although Brunel insists that there is nothing to panic about just yet.

"The [Six Nations] tournament was a disappointment," he said.

"I said it from the beginning, the World Cup is a completely different competition, reduced to four decisive matches, history has shown it to us many times. We'll have time to sort out all the details where we haven't been good, we'll try to prepare ourselves accordingly."

France's Rugby World Cup pedigree is, indeed, a positive for the side.

Finallists in 1987, 1999 and 2011, they have lit the tournament up frequently – most famously with a sublime comeback victory over New Zealand at RWC 1999.

If they can harness their undoubted talent – and nod to their attacking, competent, flair-filled past – then France can still be a huge threat in Japan. Yet, ultimately, Brunel's men have a mountain to climb to make their fourth final.

ARGENTINA

AGUSTÍN CREEVY

An international since 2005, he was expected to bid farewell to his country at the end of Rugby World Cup 2019, but has signed for two more seasons with the Unión Argentina de Rugby – confirming the hunger is still there. Originally a flanker, he shifted to hooker in 2009 in order to restart a stalled test career. He undertook his apprenticeship under current coach Mario Ledesma and captained Los Pumas to fourth place at RWC 2015. Ledesma replaced him as captain, a role he adored, but this should allow him more time to focus in what will be his third and final tournament.

MARIO LEDESMA

After doing his apprenticeship under Australia coach Michael Cheika, the veteran of four tournaments – and arguably the best at the 1999 and 2007 editions – was brought back to his country, after 17 years overseas, to head Los Jaguares, the Super Rugby franchise. Soon after, Ledesma became Puma coach for last year's Rugby Championship. As a coach, he is as straight-shooting as he was as a player and expects – and commands – fearsome respect from his charges in the dressing room. His rugby intelligence is clear for all to see and he has applied it well to aid Argentina's cause.

ENGLAND
FRANCE
ARGENTINA
USA
TONGA

POOL C

ARGENTINA
RUGBY WORLD CUP STATISTICS

World Ranking	RWC Titles	RWC Apps
10	0	8

37 MATCHES PLAYED

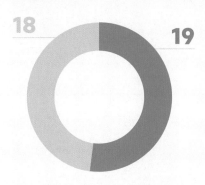

18   19

● Won   ● Lost   ● Drawn

Points scored:	Tries scored:
992	101

Average per match:	Average per match:
26.8	2.7

Conversions:	Penalties:	Drop goals:
73	107	11

Red cards:	Yellow cards:
1	10

POOL C FIXTURES

FRANCE
Sat 21 Sep, 16:15
Tokyo Stadium

TONGA
Sat 28 Sep, 13:45
Hanazono Rugby Stadium

ENGLAND
Sat 05 Oct, 17:00
Tokyo Stadium

USA
Wed 09 Oct, 13:45
Kumagaya Rugby Stadium

OVERVIEW

Facing England and France, the USA Eagles and even Tonga could constitute the 'Pool of Death' for Argentina, although there are solid arguments to say that most pools at Rugby World Cup 2019 could well fit that description.

Argentina have themselves to blame for an untimely drop in the World Rugby Rankings before pools were drawn, more so after playing for a second time in a Rugby World Cup semi-final at Twickenham four years ago, that led them to a very tough Pool C.

Yet the way they now play is a joy to see.

Soon after their success at RWC 2015, an Argentine team entered Super Rugby for the first time. Los Jaguares were born and the Unión Argentina de Rugby's policy decreed that in order to be eligible for the national team, players had to be playing Super Rugby, preferably at home.

This meant the same pool of players was used for both Los Jaguares and Los Pumas; a decision that saw the players take on a heavy workload, with mixed results.

Coach Daniel Hourcade, whose brand of open rugby had been applauded by everyone in the game, seemed to lose his touch as players were unable to rediscover the heights of England 2015 and, eventually, he resigned after a winless June window in 2018.

In came former test icon Mario Ledesma, who as assistant coach of the Wallabies had beaten Argentina at RWC 2015.

He forced changes in the selection policy, choosing players he really needed regardless of where they played, opening the door to props more than anything as the Puma scrum had been below its traditional best for a number of years.

Los Pumas beat the Springboks in his second game in charge and with a match-saving tackle in the last second from second-row Tomás Lavanini, the Wallabies were beaten in Brisbane.

It seemed that Argentina knew how to beat those Australians Ledesma had coached until a year before, but a series of disappointing results followed, ensuring nobody really knows what to expect in Japan.

The first goal, clearly, is to get out of Pool C and for that, beating France or England is crucial. While they might have the knowledge to beat the French – Ledesma played and coached for 14 years in that country – it might be harder with England. USA and Tonga may, on paper, appear to be more straightforward matches but their physicality, pride and the pressure brought on by tournament play means anything could happen.

Flanker Pablo Matera will move overseas after Japan 2019 and needs to be at his best to lead what is still a young – yet very experienced – team, with players such as tough-as-nails forwards Agustín Creevy, Marcos Kremer, Lavanini and Guido Petti in a big pack.

There is a lot of talent in the backs and they can be dangerous with ball in hand or when kicking and turning the opposition's defence. Hopefully, long-term injuries are in the past for the likes of Gonzalo Bertranou, Bautista Delguy and Emiliano Boffelli, and if Ledesma can get his first XV on the field consistently enough, Argentina will be what they always are: extremely tough to conquer.

USA

STAR MAN

JOE TAUFETE'E

Joe Taufete'e started playing rugby in Southern California to impress his high school girlfriend and her family. It worked. She married him and he's now a star for the Worcester Warriors and the USA. Taufete'e's extreme power and delicate footwork make him the USA's go-to man and he obliterated Ireland great Keith Wood's record for test tries from a front-row, surpassing Wood's 15 in only his 21st test match. USA will be tough to overcome at the breakdown at Rugby World Cup 2019 and Taufete'e is a large reason why.

COACH

GARY GOLD

With Gary Gold's appointment as head coach, the USA Eagles have found a father figure to lead them forward. After leaving his job as Director of Rugby at Worcester to head up the Eagles, the team turned around. Once he officially assumed head coach duties in 2018, Gold's Eagles won 12 of their first 14 test matches. At the centre of Gold's approach is a team ideal. He has created a coaching team that genuinely enjoys spending time together. With cohesion at the top, and a respected player leadership group, Gold has achieved impressive buy-in. Of course, winning helps, too.

ENGLAND
FRANCE
ARGENTINA
USA
TONGA

POOL C

USA
RUGBY WORLD CUP STATISTICS

World Ranking	RWC Titles	RWC Apps
15	0	7

25 MATCHES PLAYED

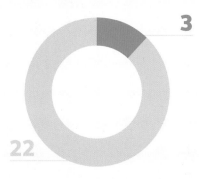

3

22

● Won ● Lost ● Drawn

Points scored:	Tries scored:
350	37

Average per match:	Average per match:
14	1.5

Conversions:	Penalties:	Drop goals:
26	38	2

Red cards:	Yellow cards:
0	8

POOL C FIXTURES

ENGLAND	FRANCE
Thurs 26 Sep, 19:45	Wed 02 Oct, 16:45
Kobe Misaki Stadium	Fukuoka Hakatanomori Stadium

ARGENTINA	TONGA
Wed 09 Oct, 13:45	Sun 13 Oct, 14:45
Kumagaya Rugby Stadium	Hanazono Rugby Stadium

OVERVIEW

The USA finished off 2018 having made history, but history has a way of catching up with you.

The Eagles recorded 10 test victories in 2018, a record for the USA team, and beat Scotland and Samoa for the first time ever – both by the score of 30-29. Add to that a second-straight Americas Rugby Championship title, this time with a perfect five wins out of five, and you see how special that year was.

Head coach Gary Gold perhaps said it best after the USA held off Scotland in Houston, asking his players: "Now do you believe me?"

Believe they did. Even in defeat the Americans had their moments. Losing to Ireland in Dublin in November wasn't much of a surprise, but to be within shouting distance at 17-14 with 30 minutes gone at least earned them respect all round.

On a high going into 2019, the Eagles started off well enough against Chile with a resounding 71-8 win. Even more important was that brilliant fly-half AJ MacGinty returned to the field after shoulder surgery and scored three tries and 25 points.

But the game also featured far too many mistakes, and a week later against an Argentina XV, those mistakes proved very costly in a 45-14 loss.

"Since we've been together just over a year now, that's our first real banana skin," said Gold.

It wasn't the last.

A victory over Brazil that was far too close for comfort, and then a loss to Uruguay a week later in which Los Teros exposed some poor tackling and a confused kicking game, brought the Eagles down to earth.

"When you're disappointed after giving up a try and you miss touch or make a handling error, that's a momentum-killer, and we've made too many of those," said Gold.

But a week later they fixed some of those issues to beat Canada 30-25 to regain some of that momentum.

Gold's Eagles enjoyed an outstanding 2018 despite the coach calling on 50 different players.

That was a symptom of a relatively unsettled few years after 2015 – new coach John Mitchell lasted 18 months, and Gold didn't take the job until six months later. While Mitchell had led the USA to a Rugby World Cup 2019 qualifier series win over Canada, the programme was still in flux.

Now, though, with all eyes focused on RWC 2019, the squad and the approach is settled.

The USA have won three RWC matches and lost 22, with 2003 (one victory and a 19-18 loss to Fiji) being the best showing.

To better that, the Eagles will call on some impressive talent – MacGinty is a top-flight fly-half, and hooker Joe Taufete'e is a monstrous talent. Paul Lasike and Bryce Campbell form a strong midfield pairing, and number eight Cam Dolan, flanker Hanco Germishuys, Blaine Scully, and second-row Nick Civetta are all seasoned pros.

Having beaten a tier one nation in Scotland, the Eagles will want to surpass 2003's performance. Beat Tonga, and then – against England, France or Argentina – they will hope to recapture a little glimmer of that 2018 glory to get an elusive second victory that will help the Eagles continue their development and also cause a seismic shock that will be felt in Japan and beyond.

TONGA

STAR MAN

SIALE PIUTAU

The captain and talisman of the national side, the winger is the longest-serving player in the current Tonga squad after making his test debut against Fiji back in 2011. He is a veteran of the 'Ikale Tahi's RWC campaigns of 2011 in New Zealand and 2015 in England, making eight appearances. At club level, the 33-year-old has represented both the Chiefs and Highlanders in Super Rugby, Counties Manukau in New Zealand provincial rugby, the Yamaha Júbilo club in Japan, as well as Wasps and Bristol in the English Premiership.

COACH

TOUTAI KEFU

The Tongan-born number eight played 60 times for Australia, making his debut from the bench against the Springboks in Pretoria in 1997. He won the Tri Nations twice with the Wallabies but the undisputed highlight of his test career came in 1999 when he started in the back-row in the Rugby World Cup final victory over France in Paris. His domestic playing career came to an end in 2010 and after coaching stints with the Sunshine Coast Stingrays, the Kubota Spears in Japan and Queensland Country, he was named the new Tonga head coach in May 2016.

ENGLAND
FRANCE
ARGENTINA
USA
TONGA

POOL C

TONGA
RUGBY WORLD CUP STATISTICS

World Ranking	RWC Titles	RWC Apps
13	0	7

25 MATCHES PLAYED

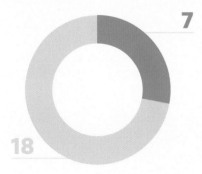

7

18

● Won ● Lost ● Drawn

Points scored:	Tries scored:
405	**44**

Average per match:	Average per match:
16.2	**1.8**

Conversions:	Penalties:	Drop goals:
28	**43**	**1**

Red cards:	Yellow cards:
3	**11**

POOL C FIXTURES

 ENGLAND
Sun 22 Sep, 19:15
Sapporo Dome

 ARGENTINA
Sat 28 Sep, 13:45
Hanazono Rugby Stadium

FRANCE
Sun 06 Oct, 16:45
Kumamoto Stadium

 USA
Sun 13 Oct, 14:45
Hanazono Rugby Stadium

OVERVIEW

Tonga head coach Toutai Kefu is nothing if not an optimist. The former Wallaby number eight has promised the 'Ikale Tahi will be "super competitive" at RWC 2019 but it's a pledge which the 45-year-old may struggle to fulfil given the raft of Tongan players he is unable to select for the tournament.

"We want to have some really good positive results at the World Cup," Kefu said. "We need to progress through to the knockout stages, we need to win three games."

That outlook is impressive, given that Kefu's squad has been shorn of up to 15 leading players he hoped to include in Japan who have either adopted different countries or are currently ineligible. Yet the Pacific Islanders are accustomed to adversity and the coach knows he can ill afford to dwell on what might have been.

Tonga are nonetheless familiar Rugby World Cup faces. They have only once failed to qualify for the tournament – in 1991 – and although they have never progressed beyond the pool stage in seven attempts, Tonga enjoy a reputation as one of the game's most dangerous and unpredictable opponents.

That was never more evident than at RWC 2011 when they faced France and pulled off a famous 19-14 win in Wellington. They will do battle with Les Bleus again this year in Kumamoto in Pool C and should they be able to repeat their heroics of eight years ago, the 'Ikale Tahi might have an outside chance of progressing beyond the pool stage.

England in Sapporo may prove a bridge too far for Kefu's side, given that they have never beaten them, but they've beaten the USA, whom they will play in Higashiōsaka in their final pool match, in their previous eight meetings. The two sides last met in San Sebastián in November 2016, a match the Tongans edged 20-17, continuing a winning run against the Americans which dates back to 1999.

That would potentially make Tonga's encounter with Argentina pivotal. The rivals have met only once previously, the Pumas winning 45-16 in Leicester at RWC 2015, but the current Argentina has had a mixed set of recent results.

They won just four times in 24 tests in 2017-18, a statistic which will not have escaped Kefu and his squad.

Tonga confirmed their eighth tournament appearance courtesy of their performances in the 2016 and 2017 World Rugby Pacific Nations Cup, qualifying alongside Fiji and condemning Samoa to a play-off against Germany.

More recently, they finished as runners-up in the four-team 2018 Pacific Nations Cup, narrowly losing 16-15 to Georgia before overcoming Samoa 28-18 in Suva.

The 'Ikale Tahi backed up that victory a week later in Lautoka, Fiji, beating the hosts 27-19 at Churchill Park.

The win ended a six-match losing streak against their old rivals which stretched back to 2011. In November last year, the Tongans were presented with a rare opportunity to face tier one opposition, when they played Wales in Cardiff, but it was a sobering outing as they succumbed to a 74-24 defeat.

Tonga will face further tier one opponents in the shape of New Zealand in Hamilton just two weeks before the start of RWC 2019 and it will be that performance against the reigning world champions that provides the litmus test for their chances of making it out of the pool stage for the first time.

aggreko

The power to win

We're proud to be Official Temporary Power Supplier for Rugby World Cup 2019™.

20 teams will do everything in their power to become world champions, but only one team will lift the Webb Ellis Cup.

It takes intelligence, expertise and above all, dedication, to be part of a victorious team – and that's something we specialise in.

Our engineering of temporary power and electrical distribution systems have been the foundation for the biggest sports events across the globe and Aggreko is ready to help Rugby World Cup 2019™ make memories for millions.

Aggreko - specialists in power, heating and cooling for world class events

Visit us at **aggreko.com** to get in touch

POOL D

Wallabies®

WRU

FLYING FIJIANS

URU

Pool D provides perhaps the biggest chance of an upset at Rugby World Cup 2019, featuring as it does three teams in the top 10 of the World Rugby Rankings. Fresh from a Six Nations Grand Slam, Wales are currently second in the world and many people's outside tip for the title, while 2015 semi-finalists Australia have the know-how to go deep into the tournament. But who can discount the mercurial Fiji, who on their day can cause anyone problems, or Georgia and Uruguay, both of whom are more than capable of causing an upset or two?

The winner of this pool will likely secure a spot in what looks the easier side of the knockout draw, so the decisive game will probably be the encounter between Australia and Wales in Tokyo on 29 September. The countries have played each other in six of the eight previous Rugby World Cups, with Wales winning the third-place play-off in 1987 before losing the next five. Wales, though, ended their long losing streak against the Wallabies in November, winning a hard-fought, try-less game to give them the psychological advantage going into RWC 2019. Warren Gatland, in his final year in charge, has developed an enviable strength in depth, while they have that magical ability to be able to nick games right at the death, and they have never been in better shape going into rugby's showpiece tournament.

Australia on the other hand, having fallen to sixth in the World Rugby Rankings, are going through something of a difficult time with coach

Michael Cheika having survived a review of his position in December after a year in which the Wallabies endured their worst set of results for 60 years. But they are one of the top performers at Rugby World Cup, winning the title twice and finishing in the top eight in every tournament since it started in 1987. And since winning their second title in 1999, they have managed to finish fourth or higher in three of the four tournaments, coming second to New Zealand last time out.

With former NRL star Semi Radradra available, a confident Ben Volavola at fly-half, a world-class second-row in Leone Nakarawa and any number of quality outside backs at their disposal, John McKee's Fiji will go into the tournament feeling like they can beat anyone. And, having beaten Wales at Rugby World Cup 2007 with a breathtaking display in what is regarded as one of rugby's great tests, their encounter at Oita Stadium on 9 October could really set this Rugby World Cup alight.

Scrummaging powerhouses Georgia will probably look to their match against Fiji on 3 October as their Rugby World Cup final, knowing that a third-place pool finish would see them qualify directly for France 2023.

Uruguay, though, who have recent experience of losing to Fiji after a 68-7 loss in November, conceded 47 points or more in each of their four defeats in 2015, and they face a tough time in trying to reduce that figure in Japan.

AUSTRALIA

MICHAEL HOOPER

It doesn't matter how poorly the Wallabies perform or how bad their results, one man never fails to give 100 per cent – captain and flanker Michael Hooper. Not tall by international standards, what Hooper lacks in size he makes up for with heart. He is the first man into the breakdown and gets through a mountain of work in defence as well as making countless metres in attack. Still just 27 – he turns 28 five days before the final of RWC 2019 – Hooper has been tasked with leading the Wallabies through some of their toughest times on and off the field, but has come through it with his head held high.

MICHAEL CHEIKA

Michael Cheika's reign as Wallabies coach started brilliantly as in his first few months in charge he took his side on a fairytale run to the RWC 2015 final, knocking out the host nation along the way. But since then plaudits have been in short supply. 2018 especially was an annus horribilis for Cheika as his side won just four of their 13 tests, with many calling for Cheika to be replaced. The former Super Rugby and European Champions Cup-winning coach however managed to hold onto his job. Time will tell if that was the right call but there is no doubt he remains a world-class coach.

AUSTRALIA
WALES
GEORGIA
FIJI
URUGUAY

POOL D

AUSTRALIA
RUGBY WORLD CUP STATISTICS

World Ranking	RWC Titles	RWC Apps
6	**2**	**8**

48 MATCHES PLAYED

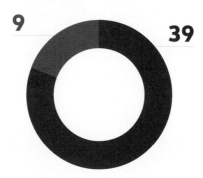

9   **39**

● Won   ● Lost   ● Drawn

Points scored:	Tries scored:
1,645	**209**
Average per match:	Average per match:
34.3	**4.4**

Conversions:	Penalties:	Drop goals:
149	**107**	**8**

Red cards:	Yellow cards:
1	**7**

POOL D FIXTURES

FIJI	WALES
Sat 21 Sep, 13:45	Sun 29 Sep, 16:45
Sapporo Dome	Tokyo Stadium
URUGUAY	GEORGIA
Sat 05 Oct, 14:15	Fri 11 Oct, 19:15
Oita Stadium	Shizuoka Stadium Ecopa

OVERVIEW

Remarkably, the Wallabies come into RWC 2019 in exactly the same position as they arrived at England 2015 – with poor on-field results and beset by off-field challenges.

Coach Michael Cheika was fortunate to hold on to his job after a disappointing run in 2018, where his side won just 30.8 per cent of their tests, but there was still a shake up to his management team, with RWC 1999 winner, and World Rugby Hall of Fame inductee, Stephen Larkham axed as attack coach and Scott Johnson brought in as the new Director of Rugby.

At the end of the last century the Wallabies were on top of the rugby world after claiming their second RWC success in Wales in 1999, thanks in part to the peerless Larkham, and the superb talents of some of the greatest Wallabies of all time such as captain John Eales and centre Tim Horan.

But Australia have failed to win any of the four tournaments since, although they did reach the final in 2003 and again surprisingly in 2015 under Cheika.

It's difficult to see them lifting the Webb Ellis Cup for a third time in Japan as just months out from RWC 2019 they are still yet to discover their best line-up and Cheika has struggled to develop any depth to his squad.

They have a number of world-class stars such as back-rows David Pocock and Michael Hooper, and the re-emergence of scrum-half Will Genia has given the Wallabies a trump card at the base of the ruck.

However, there are so many question marks over so many positions it is likely Cheika will still be experimenting as they come into their opening match against a dangerous Fiji side in Sapporo on 21 September.

Young hooker Folau Fainga'a has made the most of his chances and powerful prop Taniela Tupou, known as the Tongan Thor, has also been impressive, but neither has settled into the first choice line-up.

Cheika still depends largely on his Super Rugby winning NSW Waratahs side of 2014 for the spine of his Wallabies, but five years on the form of a number of those stars, such as fly-half Bernard Foley and playmaker Kurtley Beale, has been patchy.

The Wallabies, however, will be boosted by the return of veteran outside back Adam Ashley-Cooper, who has come back from club rugby in Japan for one last RWC campaign.

It's difficult to pinpoint why the Wallabies have slipped so far down the pecking order since RWC 2015, but in 2018 they sunk to their lowest ever World Rugby Ranking of seventh. Barring another golden run, as in England four years ago, it's hard to see them getting past Wales in Pool D, which would set up a likely meeting with former coach Eddie Jones in the quarter-finals.

Yet despite all those odds, Cheika has refused to play down Australia's chances and cannot wait for the opening match against Fiji.

"We will be in good shape when we need to be," he said. "It's going to be an open World Cup for sure – not just because of how the teams have performed leading up to here, but also because it's in Japan.

"It's going to be very different, a different atmosphere at the games. We've got a bit to do before then, but the players can't wait and the lucky ones who get picked can't wait to get on the plane."

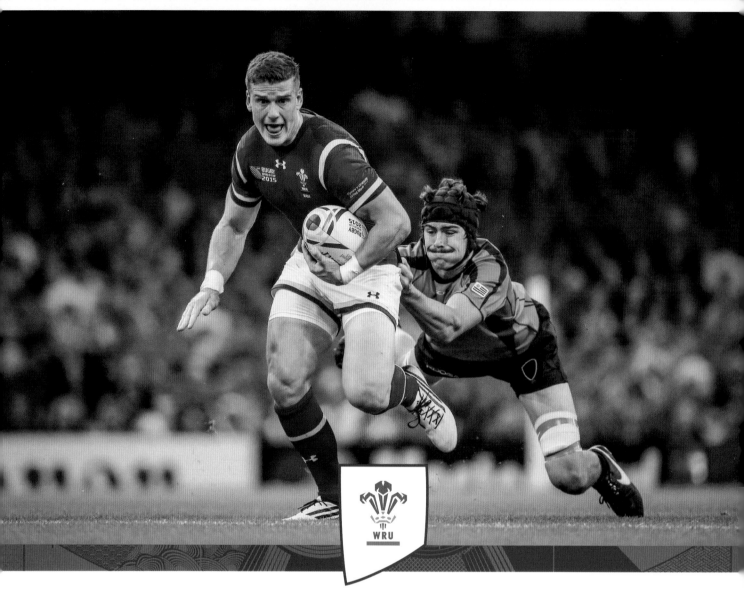

WALES

LIAM WILLIAMS

Liam Williams may describe himself as "a scaffolder living the dream" but the Welsh public must thank the day he decided to concentrate on rugby rather than working in a steel plant. Williams has the most feared trait in all of sport – blistering pace – and his mazy, twisting, jagged runs are a defender's nightmare. The Saracens winger is as happy setting up tries as he is scoring them, often providing the perfect foil for his fellow Welsh backs and, as his career progresses, he is becoming ever better at the defensive side of the game. When Williams sparks into life, Wales play brilliantly – it is as simple as that.

STAR MAN

WARREN GATLAND

Warren Gatland's 12-year reign as Wales coach will end after Rugby World Cup 2019. How they will miss him. Since his appointment, he has won a record three Grand Slams as a coach and also brilliantly guided the British and Irish Lions to a 2013 series win against Australia and a series draw against the All Blacks in 2017. Tough, uncompromising but also blessed with a wry sense of humour and respect for his opponents, Gatland has reached the pinnacle of his chosen career with a touch of class and created some dynamic, powerful and attractive rugby sides. He is certainly a legend in Wales.

COACH

AUSTRALIA
WALES
GEORGIA
FIJI
URUGUAY
POOL **D**

WALES
RUGBY WORLD CUP STATISTICS

World Ranking	RWC Titles	RWC Apps
2	**0**	**8**

37 MATCHES PLAYED

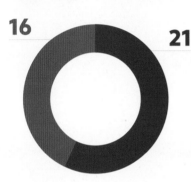

16

21

● Won ● Lost ● Drawn

Points scored:	Tries scored:
1,049	**129**
Average per match:	Average per match:
28.4	**3.5**

Conversions:	Penalties:	Drop goals:
94	**76**	**7**

Red cards:	Yellow cards:
2	**3**

POOL D FIXTURES

GEORGIA	**AUSTRALIA**
Mon 23 Sep, 19:15	Sun 29 Sep, 16:45
City of Toyota Stadium	Tokyo Stadium

FIJI	**URUGUAY**
Wed 09 Oct, 18:45	Sun 13 Oct, 17:15
Oita Stadium	Kumamoto Stadium

OVERVIEW

Wales is a rugby-fanatic country at the best of times but now, with Rugby World Cup 2019 fast approaching on the horizon, excitement across the country is reaching unprecedented levels.

And why not?

On paper, this looks like the strongest Wales team of the professional era, in the form of its life and with the best possible chance to win the one trophy that the entire nation craves more than any other.

Led by the indomitable Alun Wyn Jones, Wales' pack contains some mighty talents such as Ken Owens, Jake Ball, Taulupe Faletau, Justin Tipuric and Aaron Wainwright. The backs are just as jam-packed with style and substance as the likes of Liam Williams, George North, Jonathan Davies, Leigh Halfpenny, Dan Biggar and Gareth Anscombe are capable of giving their opponents huge trouble.

The ruthlessness and effectiveness of Warren Gatland's side is underlined by their stunning Six Nations Grand Slam earlier this year, when they swept away all in front of them to help Gatland win his third Grand Slam in just 12 years.

Against England, Wales showed all their virtues – physical commitment, composure and pace – to overcome a 10-3 half-time deficit to win 21-13; a match Welsh teams from generations past would have lost.

On their way to the Grand Slam, sealed with a comfortable last day victory over Ireland, Wales set a new record for consecutive victories – an incredible 14 straight wins – and Gatland's side look as if they have simply forgotten how to lose.

It is that ability to reach deep inside themselves and find the necessary skills required to win a match that means Wales go into RWC 2019 in a confident mood and they are strong candidates to repeat England's feat at RWC 2003 and bring the Webb Ellis Cup to the northern hemisphere.

Gatland is never a man to get too over-excited by rugby and takes the wins and losses in a phlegmatic, laidback manner.

Yet he would not be human if he was not especially looking forward to Japan as he looks to end his tenure as Wales coach with a tournament victory that would truly seal his place in Welsh sporting folklore.

"I know that these guys won't go down in any match without a fight," he said.

"We've got a very special group of players at the moment. We enjoy each other's company, we challenge each other on a lot of things, but once we make a decision we back each other 100 per cent. You need a little bit of luck and hopefully we don't pick up too many injuries.

"We'll have a few months of preparation and, as we have in the last few World Cups, we'll be one of the fittest teams, if not the fittest team there.

"I assure you that we'll go there with some confidence and belief that we can have a great World Cup."

Wales have been a huge threat at previous Rugby World Cups, making the semi-finals in 1987 and 2011, and the quarter-finals on three other occasions.

Yet the sense that they have never fulfilled their potential at the highest level remains justified.

However, thanks to this squad – and Gatland – that could all change in Japan.

GEORGIA

VASIL LOBZHANIDZE

Georgia's pack have previously taken all the plaudits, but with a more expansive style of play the backs are now enjoying their time in the spotlight. Vasil Lobzhandize is a perfect example, having established himself as Georgia's first-choice scrum-half in recent years. Lobzhanidze wrote his name into the RWC history books when, at England 2015, he became the youngest player in the tournament's history at 18 years and 340 days against Tonga. Lobzhanidze, who currently plays for Brive in the Top 14, already has more than 40 caps at the age of 22, and is as passionate as they come.

MILTON HAIG

Having been a decent player in New Zealand and beyond, Milton Haig's coaching career began in 1991 when he took up a player/coach role with Greerton Marist RFC between 1991 and 1993. He also had a spell in Scotland and was then player/coach for Mount Maunganui RFC. Between 2003 and 2011 he was involved with all New Zealand age-grade teams and the Maori All Blacks. In 2011 he was handed the top role with Georgia and has enjoyed his time with them since, turning them into a formidable opponent on the world stage. They finished third in their pool at Rugby World Cup 2015 to qualify for this showpiece event.

AUSTRALIA
WALES
GEORGIA
FIJI
URUGUAY

POOL D

GEORGIA
RUGBY WORLD CUP STATISTICS

World Ranking	RWC Titles	RWC Apps
12	0	4

16 MATCHES PLAYED

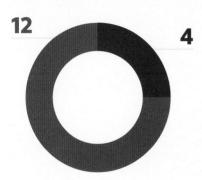

12 ● Won   **4**

● Won   ● Lost   ● Drawn

Points scored:	Tries scored:
197	**15**

Average per match:	Average per match:
12.3	**0.9**

Conversions:	Penalties:	Drop goals:
14	**32**	**1**

Red cards:	Yellow cards:
0	**7**

POOL D FIXTURES

WALES
Mon 23 Sep, 19:15
City of Toyota Stadium

URUGUAY
Sun 29 Sep, 14:15
Kumagaya Rugby Stadium

FIJI
Thu 03 Oct, 14:15
Hanazono Rugby Stadium

AUSTRALIA
Fri 11 Oct, 19:15
Shizuoka Stadium Ecopa

OVERVIEW

Finishing third in their pool at Rugby World Cup 2015 was a big result for Georgia and meant they could build towards this tournament without the fear of missing out or having to go through a gruelling qualification process.

That good showing sent them into 2016 on a high and they started very strongly, winning all five games to see them win the Rugby Europe Championship.

They lost the 2017 Rugby Europe Championship to Romania but won 10 Championship matches in a row to lift the trophy in both 2018 and 2019, and they will be feeling good heading into Rugby World Cup 2019.

Coach Milton Haig has worked wonders in his adopted homeland and is a widely revered figure throughout Georgia, and beyond.

Despite speculation linking him with other international coaching positions, Haig has taken Georgia to his heart, moving his family with him to the country and embracing the culture and lifestyle.

More importantly than that, he has moulded a squad of superb rugby players; physically imposing and wonderfully gifted.

Georgia's style is more practical than pretty, based on a tremendously strong and well-drilled pack, overseen by former England prop Graham Rowntree.

The likes of Beka Gigashvili, Shalva Mamukashvili, Nodar Cheishvili and Beka Gorgadze are brilliantly strong and gifted in the scrum while scrum-half Vasil Lobzhanidze and fly-half Tedo Abzhandadze do a sterling job in leading Georgia around the field.

The pride Georgia's players feel in representing their nation is visible to all when they take the field and after qualifying for RWC 2019 in such fine style in England four years ago, Haig explained how rugby continues to blossom as Georgia's most popular sport.

"You couldn't walk into any place without people coming up and congratulating us. It wasn't happening occasionally, it was everywhere we went. As a result the popularity of the game has just kept on going and going," he said.

"The people have recognised the values of the game, the respect among players to the opposition and officials. These are big men battling on the field but off the field they share a drink with each other and have a chat. The locals haven't seen anything like that before."

In terms of this showpiece event, Georgia have been involved at every Rugby World Cup since 2003.

They did not win a game in the pool stages 16 years ago, but at RWC 2007 they recorded their first tournament victory over Namibia, and gave Ireland a fright in a 14-10 defeat.

At RWC 2011 their journey was ended in the pool stage despite picking up another positive result, this time a 25-9 victory over Romania.

Four years later and wins over Tonga and Namibia in the pool stage saw them finish third behind New Zealand and Argentina.

So, what of Georgia's hopes this time?

Well, they have a good chance of beating both Fiji and Uruguay, but it looks likely that they will have to topple either Australia or Wales to make it through to the last eight for the first time.

And if that happens, Haig and his men will be more popular than ever.

FIJI

STAR MAN

SEMI RADRADRA

There was much excitement in the Pacific Islands when blockbusting back Semi Radradra was tempted from Australian rugby league to join French club Bordeaux Bègles in 2017, in a move that made him eligible for selection for his home nation. Some players changing codes have failed to deliver but not the 26-year-old flyer, who has lived up to all expectations for club and country in both 15s and sevens. Nicknamed "Semi-Trailer", Radradra's rampaging try in November last year set up Fiji's 21-14 win over France, their first ever victory over Les Bleus in 15s. Expect more of the same at Rugby World Cup 2019.

COACH

JOHN McKEE

Taking over as head coach of the Flying Fijians in February 2014, former AS Montferrand and Connacht coach John McKee has led the proud Pacific nation to one of the most successful periods in their history. Known for clever tactical nous and shrewd player management, New Zealand-born McKee was tasked with taking Fiji to their highest ever World Rugby Ranking of eighth and he achieved that task in 2018, holding the position into this year. McKee has built an impressive squad with considerable depth, who have now developed some stability at the set-piece to go with their famous flair.

AUSTRALIA
WALES
GEORGIA
FIJI
URUGUAY

FIJI
RUGBY WORLD CUP STATISTICS

World Ranking	RWC Titles	RWC Apps
9	**0**	**7**

28 MATCHES PLAYED

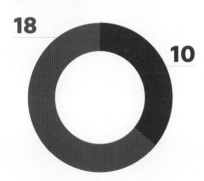

18

10

● Won   ● Lost   ● Drawn

Points scored:	Tries scored:
622	**70**

Average per match:	Average per match:
22.2	**2.5**

Conversions:	Penalties:	Drop goals:
53	**54**	**6**

Red cards:	Yellow cards:
1	**9**

POOL D FIXTURES

AUSTRALIA
Sat 21 Sep, 13:45
Sapporo Dome

URUGUAY
Wed 25 Sep, 14:15
Kamaishi Recovery
Memorial Stadium

GEORGIA
Thu 03 Oct, 14:15
Hanazono Rugby
Stadium

WALES
Wed 09 Oct, 18:45
Oita Stadium

OVERVIEW

For many years Fiji have been known for their thrilling style of play, with outrageous passes and flying runners lighting up rugby fields around the world.

But where Fiji have often been let down in 15s rugby is the set-piece and being unable to sustain a level of performance over a full 80 minutes.

However, under the composed guidance of New Zealander John McKee since 2014, Fiji have developed a maturity and discipline that now sees them challenging the best in the world.

McKee's subtle transformation reached its high point on 24 November last year, in Paris no less, when the Flying Fijians completely outplayed France to claim a first-ever victory over the Six Nations heavyweights in 60 years of trying.

What made the loss even harder for Les Bleus was the fact that Fiji's destroyers on the night all play their club rugby in France, try-scorers Semi Radradra (Bordeaux Bègles) and Josua Tuisova (Toulon), and Ben Volavola (Racing 92), who added a conversion and three penalties.

However, the victory was built on a powerhouse performance by the Fijian pack, which boasts one of their strongest ever tight fives: second-rows Leone Nakarawa and Tevita Cavubati, props Manasa Saulo and Campese Ma'afu, with hooker Sam Matavesi.

This is backed up by an impressive back-row of number eight Viliame Mata and flankers Peceli Yato and captain Dominiko Waqaniburotu.

With that pack winning a steady supply of possession, the Fijian backline, which also includes Harlequins speedster Vereniki Goneva and Bayonne's Metuisela Talebula, will test any defence.

As McKee said on the famous night in Paris: "It's a massive achievement. We told each other this week that if we beat France we would make it into the pantheon of Fijian rugby."

The result, however, was no fluke as Fiji have defeated other Six Nations teams in recent years, including Italy in both 2014 (McKee's first game in charge) and 2017, and a memorable victory over Scotland, also in 2017.

The current sevens Olympic champions, Fiji have also dominated Pacific rugby in recent years, claiming the World Rugby Pacific Nations Cup for the last four seasons, while the Fijian Drua development side won Australia's National Rugby Championship in 2018.

But Fiji will be setting their sights even higher in Japan where they will hope to return to the quarter-finals for the first time since their memorable run in France in 2007, where they threatened to knock eventual winners South Africa out in the last eight.

This was Fiji's second trip to the knockout rounds after also reaching the quarter-finals in the very first RWC in New Zealand in 1987.

In a curious quirk of fate, Pool D at RWC 2019 has four of the five teams from Pool A in England four years earlier, with the only change, Georgia, in for the 2015 hosts.

In that tournament, Fiji were well beaten by England, Australia and Wales but in Japan they will be more than hopeful of reaching the last eight.

URUGUAY

SANTIAGO ARATA

Santiago Arata is one of those players who can do things on a rugby field that others wouldn't even think of. From an early age, even before rugby was to become what it has in his country, he had the will to play at the highest level. Turning 23 in early September, he will arrive in Japan on the back of four seasons of test rugby and one season as a professional in the USA, where he played for Major League Rugby's Houston SaberCats. His pacy, aggressive style fits modern rugby and he has been crucial in transforming Uruguay into a flowing, open side.

STANDMAN

ESTEBAN MENESES

For Esteban Meneses, Japan will be his first Rugby World Cup. A rangy, efficient club player for La Plata, in Buenos Aires' first division, he had a stint in Italian rugby before his rugby brain was put to good use back home. When Uruguayan hero Pablo Lemoine stepped down, Meneses was brought to Montevideo to coach for what have been four very successful seasons. The growing Americas Rugby Championship, the popular Nations Cup and test windows have helped him prepare Los Teros into a mature and confident group of players.

COACH

AUSTRALIA
WALES
GEORGIA
FIJI
URUGUAY

POOL D

URUGUAY
RUGBY WORLD CUP STATISTICS

World Ranking	RWC Titles	RWC Apps
19	0	3

11 MATCHES PLAYED

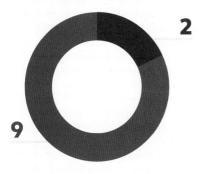

2
9

● Won ● Lost ● Drawn

Points scored:	Tries scored:
128	**12**

Average per match:	Average per match:
11.6	**1.1**

Conversions:	Penalties:	Drop goals:
7	**18**	**0**

Red cards:	Yellow cards:
1	**2**

POOL D FIXTURES

 FIJI
Wed 25 Sep, 14:15
Kamaishi Recovery
Memorial Stadium

 GEORGIA
Sun 29 Sep, 14:15
Kumagaya Rugby
Stadium

 AUSTRALIA
Sat 05 Oct, 14:15
Oita Stadium

 WALES
Sun 13 Oct, 17:15
Kumamoto Stadium

OVERVIEW

For a team such as Uruguay, to qualify 20 months before they open their campaign against Fiji on 25 September, in what promises to be an emotional afternoon at the Kamaishi Recovery Memorial Stadium, was a real luxury. They beat Canada home and away in January and February of 2018, giving coach Esteban Meneses and his squad time to prepare every aspect of their campaign.

It is fair to say that Los Teros' road to the city that has risen back after the horrific tsunami of a few years back, began way before they secured their place in Pool D.

Ten years ago, a derelict soccer stadium, Estadio Charrúa, was offered to the Uruguayan Rugby Union in the leafy Carrasco district of Montevideo. The challenge of getting it back up to scratch was taken and after taking possession in January 2012, day by day, with the muscle and brains of a united rugby community, it became one of the best rugby high performance centres in South America. And directly responsible for Los Teros playing their second consecutive Rugby World Cup.

The vision was accompanied by the support of World Rugby in terms of finance, technical assistance and competition. Funding also came from the national government and sponsors that found in the game values missing elsewhere in society.

Hungry players, intelligent coaches – previously Pablo Lemoine, now Meneses – the recipe for success was there.

Hosting international tournaments at home helped Los Teros win the World Rugby Nations Cup in 2017, 2018 and 2019 and end last year beating Romania in Bucharest, a team they had always struggled to beat.

Their RWC 2019 goal will be to perform at their highest possible standard but playing against three top 10-ranked teams is set to be a huge challenge. As they always do, they will tackle it head first, giving 100 per cent. Winning their first game since their RWC debut against Spain in 1999 would be their Rugby World Cup final.

There is a good blend of players, mixing youth and experience with players such as second-row Diego Magno, the most capped Tero, number eight Alejandro Nieto and captain Juan Manuel Gaminara, all now seasoned internationals.

Fly-half Felipe Berchesi has also honed his huge skills, and polished boot, in French rugby for the past five years and will have inside of him the mercurial Santiago Arata, a rare talent that if given half an inch, will dumbfound defences.

Argentina-born coach Meneses' gentle demeanour belies the inner grit he brings to the team. He has instilled in them a belief that anything can happen and has created a team that plays in an attacking style, no longer based on a strong pack and a kicking fly-half.

Where Uruguay will have to improve before they face Fiji is in and around the scrum, where they are often out-maneouvred by more experienced packs.

A solid base, and fewer penalties, would be a huge boost for Meneses' side and should be what they spend most time working on in the build-up to RWC 2019. If Uruguay can fix that issue then they certainly have enough desire, talent and heart to cause real problems in Japan.

THE WEBB ELLIS CUP GOES GLOBAL

RWC 2019 Trophy Tour brings rugby to the world

"Rugby World Cup represents all that we aspire to in terms of excellence, friendship and respect and we know that having the Webb Ellis Cup here will have helped reinforce those values and inspired many of our players, young and old."

Those were the words of HKRU CEO Robbie McRobbie as the Rugby World Cup 2019 Trophy Tour reached Hong Kong last year.

The Webb Ellis Cup has travelled the globe, helping to promote rugby in areas of the world where the sport is already deeply embedded, and others where the game continues to grow.

The glittering trophy left the World Rugby Hall of Fame in England late in 2017 and has found its way to Uruguay, China, France, India and Canada, among other places, on a 19-country tour before landing in Japan in time for the 100 days to go celebrations.

It has visited the Taj Mahal, the Great Wall of China and Taal Volcano in the Philippines and it has helped to draw many people to our fantastic sport.

World Rugby Chairman Sir Bill Beaumont said: "The Rugby World Cup 2019 Trophy Tour plays a major role in promoting and celebrating rugby in markets that are of strategic importance to the growth of the game, while also providing a platform to showcase the excellent Impact Beyond 2019 legacy programme, that is welcoming more than one million new participants to the sport in Asia."

"To have the Rugby World Cup 2019 Trophy Tour grace our shores and pay a personal visit to Rugby House is indeed a huge honour and a very important one as it reminds us of what is at stake in Japan"

Fiji Rugby CEO John O'Connor

"The arrival of the Webb Ellis Cup in the host nation is a symbolic moment for fans, kicking off the final countdown to the tournament. It is extra special on this occasion as Japan 2019 is the first Rugby World Cup in Asia"

World Rugby Chief Executive Brett Gosper

"It is fantastic to see the impact the famous Webb Ellis Cup has had around the world, energising fans young and old and inspiring people to pick up a ball for the first time"

World Rugby Chairman Sir Bill Beaumont

"Children as young as five can see just how special the Rugby World Cup is and it was a unique opportunity to coach in the surroundings of the Great Wall alongside the Webb Ellis Cup"

Han Xiaolong, a coach with the China Rugby Football Association

"The Rugby World Cup means a lot not only to the rugby community across the world but to us at Philippine Rugby. We've been to the Rugby World Cup Sevens and our mission for the national team is to get to the Rugby World Cup in the 15-a-side game"

Philippine Rugby General Manager Jake Letts (pictured, below)

RUGBY WORLD CUP 2019 TROPHY TOUR

England	Ireland
Uruguay	Malaysia
Spain	Germany
Fiji	South Africa
Hong Kong	USA
China	Canada
The Philippines	Brazil
India	Chile
France	Argentina
Nepal	Japan

GETTING IT RIGHT

Referee Nigel Owens lifts the lid on what it takes to officiate at a Rugby World Cup, how the role continues to develop and his excitement about RWC 2019

Nigel Owens has built a formidable reputation as the world's most experienced referee, with a record 90 test matches in the middle before the start of this Rugby World Cup, thanks to a distinctive mix of rigour and relaxed empathy with the players.

The popular Welshman is grateful for everything he has gained from this often pressurised profession, and he is enthusiastic about the ways in which he and his colleagues have been obliged to move with the times.

"I can think of two obvious areas in which international refereeing has evolved," the 48-year-old Owens says, as he looks forward to his fourth Rugby World Cup with the whistle, including the ultimate honour of handling the final at RWC 2015.

"One is on the field, with the change of touch judges to becoming assistant referees, and the introduction of TMOs [television match officials] and technology – so instead of having one pair of eyes to judge things, we now have four.

"The game is becoming faster all the time, and refereeing of these big occasions and incidents is a little easier when you can rely on technology – but also there is more pressure because people expect you to get every single decision right, and they are scrutinising every one.

"And a lot of decisions in rugby are 50-50 ones where you could give a penalty, or not, and you'd be right in both circumstances.

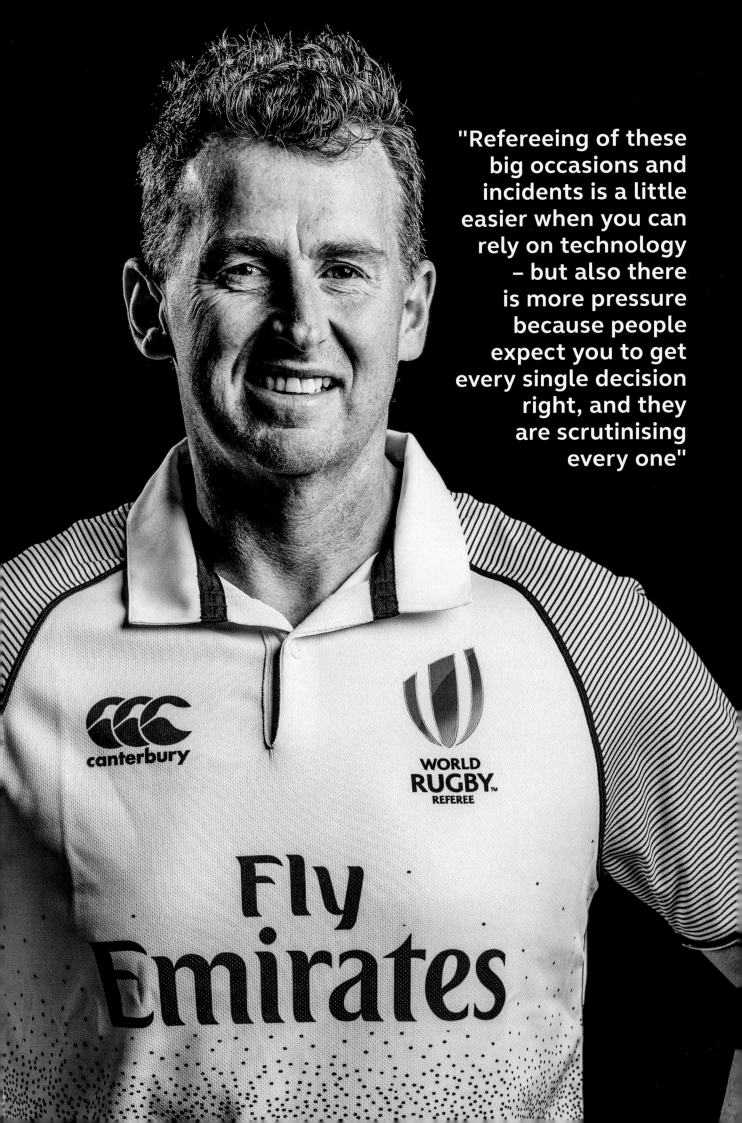

"Refereeing of these big occasions and incidents is a little easier when you can rely on technology – but also there is more pressure because people expect you to get every single decision right, and they are scrutinising every one"

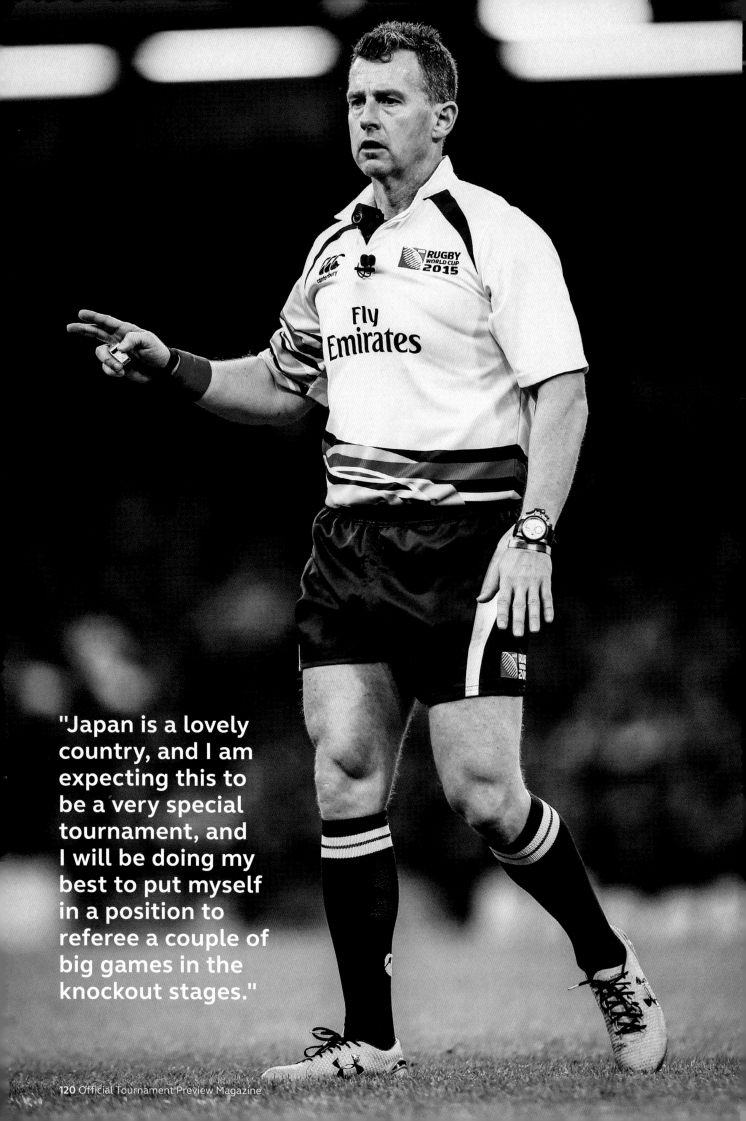

"Japan is a lovely country, and I am expecting this to be a very special tournament, and I will be doing my best to put myself in a position to referee a couple of big games in the knockout stages."

"Off the field, the game is much more professional for referees – the fitness and the training and preparation has improved hugely since I started out as a teenager. I remember when I was touch judge for Chris White [the long-serving English referee] at a match in South Africa in the early 2000s, and the first time I met Chris was when we arrived at Heathrow Airport to catch the flight out there!

"Now the referees meet in camps before or during the main competitions – an example being the three-day mini-camp we had in Japan in July this year – and we were due to get together for 10 days before the Rugby World Cup itself. That's why I think you see a good amount of consistency in refereeing now; we are all working as a team."

Owens' humorous asides to players – almost always off the cuff – can be relived on YouTube, and as a some-time television presenter and speaker in schools and other events, he is a willing and able participant in our age of superb television match coverage and multiple replays.

He also embraces the opportunity to comment on his own and other referees' decisions by using social media.

"A lot of people have said to me they have found my comments helpful – not necessarily in clarifying a particular decision, but in clarifying the laws so people can understand the decision, or so they can understand the laws better and decide themselves," he said.

"You sometimes read comments online about a decision, and you think 'oh hang on now, the referee was actually 100 per cent correct'. In a complex game like rugby, I do think it's important we try to educate people around what it's like to be a referee, and around the laws of the game, and if people understand better they can be more realistic in their comments.

"And, even if their side might have lost, there is no point in them slagging off the referee."

Owens has seen the advent of professional players making the switch to refereeing, and he speculates that TMOs may join referees and their assistants as full-time officials by the time we get to France for RWC 2023.

First, though, there is Japan and Owens says: "What I have found when I have been to Japan is the people were very polite and respectful, for the opposition team and for the referee – you never heard booing in the stadium.

"It is a lovely country, and I am expecting this to be a very special tournament, and I will be doing my best to put myself in a position to referee a couple of big games in the knockout stages."

RWC 2019 OFFICIALS

REFEREES
Wayne Barnes (England), Nic Berry (Australia), Jérôme Garcès (France), Angus Gardner (Australia), Pascal Gaüzère (France), Ben O'Keeffe (New Zealand), Nigel Owens (Wales), Luke Pearce (England), Jaco Peyper (S Africa), Romain Poite (France), Mathieu Raynal (France), Paul Williams (New Zealand)

ASSISTANT REFEREES
Federico Anselmi (Argentina), Andrew Brace (Ireland), Matthew Carley (England, reserve referee), Karl Dickson (England), Shuhei Kubo (Japan), Brendon Pickerill (New Zealand), Alex Ruiz (France)

TELEVISION MATCH OFFICIALS
Graham Hughes (England), Marius Jonker (S Africa), Rowan Kitt (England), Ben Skeen (New Zealand)

TOURNAMENT LEGACY

RWC 2019 will be a game-changer for rugby in Japan, Asia and around the globe

A decade ago when Japan was awarded the right to host Rugby World Cup 2019, it was decided to bring the sport's showpiece tournament to Asia for the first time with one vitally important goal at its heart – to use the inspiration of the tournament to create a lasting legacy for rugby across Asia.

The World Rugby Council believed that Japan 2019 could be a powerful driver for sporting and social change in Asia, the world's most populous and youthful continent. This has proven to be the case and 10 years later the tournament is set to become the most impactful Rugby World Cup in history.

> **"The World Rugby Council believed that Japan 2019 could be a powerful driver for sporting and social change in Asia, the world's most populous and youthful continent"**

With the most accessible and affordable ticketing programme to date, and matches taking place from Sapporo in the north to Kumamoto in the south – with 70 per cent of the population within one hour of a match venue – everyone is welcome at Japan 2019, keeping true to World Rugby's vision of a sport for all.

Key to World Rugby's ambition for Japan 2019 is the Impact Beyond legacy programme.

The initiative has surpassed all expectations by achieving its remarkable target of inspiring more than one million new rugby participants across Asia by the end of 2018.

Launched in 2013, the ground-breaking Impact Beyond programme is a central pillar in World Rugby's mission to grow the game globally, providing opportunities for men, women, boys and girls to be introduced to the game around the world.

The programme has had a tremendous impact across Asia, with huge numbers of players experiencing the sport in emerging rugby nations such as Pakistan (237,000), China (180,000) and India (106,000), as well as many players from diverse age, gender, ethnic and social backgrounds having their first taste of rugby in countries such as Bangladesh, the Philippines, Malaysia, Nepal, Sri Lanka and Indonesia.

An important element of World Rugby's legacy plan is a commitment to bringing positive social change through the power of sport.

Thanks to the generosity of the global rugby family and Rugby World Cup 2019 Worldwide Partners, more than 25,000 underprivileged children and youths, from Laos, the Philippines, Vietnam and other Asian countries, have benefitted from participation in the ChildFund Pass It Back programme, an innovative sport for development programme in partnership with World Rugby, which integrates life skills and rugby.

Perhaps the most profound tournament legacy is the new stadium that has been constructed in Kamaishi, acting as a beacon of hope and bringing a renewed sense of optimism and regeneration to a region so tragically devastated by the 2011 Tsunami.

The tournament legacy is also a story of human development as thousands of volunteers have been trained and learnt new skills. Many of them will take their Rugby World Cup experience and go on to become the faces of the Tokyo 2020 Olympic and Paralympic Games and apply their new skills in communities across Japan for many years to come.

The tournament legacy will also be felt in the pockets of businesses and employees around Japan. Rugby World Cup 2019 is set to deliver record economic benefits as an economic impact study revealed that Japan 2019 is set to deliver nearly ¥216.6 billion (£1.5 billion) of additive value into the Japanese economy.

The hosting of the tournament will also help support a wide range of job opportunities across different sectors for a variety of different demographics of the population. The report conducted by international consultancy EY estimates that up to 25,000 jobs will be supported across the country.

There has never been a more exciting time for rugby in Asia with fan-engagement, broadcast audiences and player participation numbers growing year-on-year. Asia is at the centre of rugby's global growth success story and Rugby World Cup 2019 is set to be a fantastic celebration of the emergence of rugby across the continent.

TOUR WITH US. THE LIONS.

This is your chance to be part of rugby's ultimate touring experience...

Buy your Priority Access Pass now and be at the front of the queue to join the British & Irish Lions in South Africa 2021.

Buy now at lionsrugby.com/tours

TOUR WITH US. THE LIONS.

SA
2021

INVESTING IN THE FUTURE COMPETITIVENESS OF THE SPORT

World Rugby is committed to a sustainable legacy of global growth

Rugby World Cup has a habit of creating unforgettable underdog moments that upset the form book and capture the hearts of fans around the world. Think 'the miracle of Brighton' in 2015 when Japan defeated South Africa, Fiji beating Wales to book a quarter-final spot in 2007, Tonga defeating eventual 2011 finalists France or Georgia securing automatic qualification through impressive form in 2015.

Each are the result of meticulous planning, and incredible character and talent, but they are also helped along the way by a targeted programme of investment in high-performance programmes and competitions that, in part, enables the emerging rugby nations to perform to their potential, and sometimes above their potential, at Rugby World Cup.

As the international federation for the sport, World Rugby is committed to the global growth of the game. In short, it wants as many teams to be as sustainably competitive as possible to inspire new fans and create new investment opportunities.

In getting to Rugby World Cup 2019, most of the emerging nations will have received a considerable level of support underpinned by a £61 million investment in direct and indirect union funding over the four-year cycle, a 22 per cent increase on the previous Rugby World Cup cycle.

This dedicated investment includes tailored high-performance programmes, including targeted coaching staff – 120 of the 150 coaches involved in emerging nation matches in November 2018 were either funded or sourced by World Rugby.

The programme also includes underwriting additional assembly time costs, strength and conditioning, specialist coaching and medical staff, dedicated elite competitions such as the Pacific Nations Cup and Nations Cup and the Fijian Drua's participation in the National Rugby Championship in Australia – all geared towards optimal performance at Japan 2019.

Looking ahead to Rugby World Cup 2023 in France, World Rugby has developed a programme of fixtures within the 2020-32 calendar that will see a record 139 tier one versus tier two tests with the Pacific Islands, Georgia, USA and Japan among the unions set to welcome the world's biggest teams for test matches or test series. All of this is geared towards ensuring the very best platform possible to compete against, and beat, the best teams in the world.

"IT WAS A PINCH YOURSELF MOMENT"

Two-time Rugby World Cup winning legend John Eales speaks about his pride at being a World Rugby Hall of Fame inductee and why everybody should take the opportunity to visit

While the greatest players of today may all be heading to Japan to try and fulfill their rugby dreams, the greatest from eras past also have their own place to visit, contemplate and enjoy their own contributions to rugby's rich, unique heritage.

The World Rugby Hall of Fame, based in the town of Rugby, lets fans take a glimpse into the game's past, celebrate the present and get excited about the future.

Based at the Rugby Art Gallery and Museum in the town since November 2016, the World Rugby Hall of Fame brings the game to life.

The latest HD touch-screen technology helps outline the values that make the sport so unique and interactive displays even allow visitors to test their hand-eye co-ordination to see if they have what it takes to be a future rugby great.

Rugby's rich history is also explored in-depth, tracing the sport's journey back to the day William Webb Ellis first picked up a football and ran with it at Rugby School in 1823.

World Rugby first created a Hall of Fame in 2006 – indeed, Webb Ellis was the first person inducted – and its annual ceremony is now one of rugby's most notable events as the latest players to be admitted to the Hall of Fame get announced and acclaimed.

Since its inception, the Hall of Fame has welcomed the likes of Gareth Edwards, Rob Andrew, Maggie Alphonsi, Serge Blanco, Agustín Pichot, John Smit and Yoshihiro Sakata.

"It was a great honour, a great thrill and a big surprise. I've always appreciated rugby's past and its heritage and visiting the Hall of Fame was a great experience"

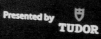

HALL *of* FAME

CELEBRATING RUGBY'S GREATEST

WHERE TO BUY TICKETS
Tickets can be purchased in person and online.
To purchase online, please visit:
www.world.rugby/halloffame/visit

OPENING TIMES
Located in Rugby, UK
Monday–Saturday: 10:00-17:00
Sunday: 10:00-16:00

WORLD RUGBY™
HALL *of* **FAME**

Presented by

TUDOR

It is not just players who are invited with open arms either.

Included amongst the roll-call you will find the 1920 United States Olympic team, the 1888 British Lions and even Rugby School itself, a fellow inaugural inductee alongside the aforementioned Webb Ellis.

One man who helps decide which candidates get chosen to join one of sport's most exclusive clubs is John Eales, a Rugby World Cup winner in 1991 with

Australia and again, as Wallabies captain, in 1999.

Rightly regarded as one of the most influential and outstanding second-rows in history – and also a wonderful leader of his country – Eales became a Hall of Fame inductee in 2007 and remains humbled by his inclusion in a list of players regarded as the very best in rugby history.

Eales now also serves as chairman of the Hall of Fame panel and visited Rugby last September to welcome Ronan O'Gara, Liza Burgess, Stephen Larkham, Pierre Villepreux and Bryan Williams to the prestigious group.

Each inductee is given a special pin and cap to recognise their contributions to the game and they usually share Eales' astonishment at being saluted in such a memorable fashion.

"I never even believed I'd play for my country," Eales said. "And then you get to do that and that is such an overwhelming experience. You don't play rugby simply to get inducted into a Hall of Fame – you play for your team-mates and your country but it was still a great honour, a great thrill and a big surprise.

"It is humbling and it was one of those pinch yourself moments."

Eales was really impressed by his visit and wryly remembered the last time he had been in the area.

"I had the opportunity to visit Rugby when I was with the Emerging Wallabies tour in 1990 and we actually trained on the fields at Rugby School," he said.

"That was a long time ago now! I've always appreciated rugby's past and its heritage and visiting the Hall of Fame was a great experience.

"To be back in the area after so long and to be visiting such an important place was very special."

rugbyworldcup.com
#RWC2019 [facebook] [twitter] [youtube] [instagram]

JOIN THE CONVERSATION

Head over to our various social media channels to share your experiences of Rugby World Cup 2019

Follow @rugbyworldcup and tag your content #RWC2019

Rugby World Cup 2019 is shaping up to be the biggest tournament yet, and we want you to get involved. For extensive match coverage, live updates and the best of video head over to our Twitter channel. Match highlights, player features, live streaming, 360 videos and more can be found on our Facebook channel, while Instagram will give you behind the scenes access like never before. Dancing fans, player reactions and the best stories of each match day will be covered on Giphy and our newly launched Rugby World Cup TikTok channel. Wherever you're watching in the world, share your experiences with the global rugby community.

Download on the App Store

GET IT ON Google Play

GET THE APP!

MATCH HASHTAGS

POOL A
#JPNvRUS
#IREvSCO
#RUSvSAM
#JPNvIRE
#SCOvSAM
#IREvRUS
#JPNvSAM
#SCOvRUS
#IREvSAM
#JPNvSCO

POOL B
#NZLvRSA
#ITAvNAM
#ITAvCAN
#RSAvNAM
#NZLvCAN
#RSAvITA
#NZLvNAM
#RSAvCAN
#NZLvITA
#NAMvCAN

POOL C
#FRAvARG
#ENGvTGA
#ENGvUSA
#ARGvTGA
#FRAvUSA
#ENGvARG
#FRAvTGA
#ARGvUSA
#ENGvFRA
#USAvTGA

POOL D
#AUSvFIJ
#WALvGEO
#FIJvURU
#GEOvURU
#AUSvWAL
#GEOvFIJ
#AUSvURU
#WALvFIJ
#AUSvGEO
#WALvURU

STATS ENTERTAINMENT

The facts and figures that matter from the eight editions of Rugby World Cup so far

WALL OF FAME

Most points scored	Jonny Wilkinson	England	277
Most points scored in a match	Simon Culhane New Zealand v Japan, RWC 1995	New Zealand	45
Most tries scored	Jonah Lomu	New Zealand	15
	Bryan Habana	South Africa	15
Most tries scored in a match	Marc Ellis New Zealand v Japan, RWC 1995	New Zealand	6
Most conversions	Dan Carter	New Zealand	58
Most conversions in a match	Simon Culhane New Zealand v Japan, RWC 1995	New Zealand	20
Most penalties	Jonny Wilkinson	England	58
Most drop goals	Jonny Wilkinson	England	14
Most drop goals in a match	Jannie de Beer South Africa v England, RWC 1999	South Africa	5
Most matches	Jason Leonard	England	22
	Richie McCaw	New Zealand	22

1987 TOURNAMENT STATS

POOL STAGE - FINAL STANDINGS

POOL A

Team	Wins	Draws	Losses	For	Against	Tries	Points
Australia	3	0	0	108	41	18	6
England	2	0	1	100	32	15	4
USA	1	0	2	39	99	5	2
Japan	0	0	3	48	123	7	0

*Australia and England advanced to the quarter-finals

POOL B

Team	Wins	Draws	Losses	For	Against	Tries	Points
Wales	3	0	0	82	31	13	6
Ireland	2	0	1	84	41	11	4
Canada	1	0	2	65	90	8	2
Tonga	0	0	3	29	98	3	0

*Wales and Ireland advanced to the quarter-finals

POOL C

Team	Wins	Draws	Losses	For	Against	Tries	Points
New Zealand	3	0	0	190	34	30	6
Fiji	1	0	2	56	101	6	2
Italy	1	0	2	40	110	5	2
Argentina	1	0	2	49	90	4	2

*New Zealand and Fiji advanced to the quarter-finals
Fiji qualified ahead of Italy and Argentina by scoring more tries

POOL D

Team	Wins	Draws	Losses	For	Against	Tries	Points
France	2	1	0	145	44	25	5
Scotland	2	1	0	135	69	22	5
Romania	1	0	2	61	130	6	2
Zimbabwe	0	0	3	53	151	5	0

*France and Scotland advanced to the quarter-finals
France qualified ahead of Scotland by scoring more tries

FACTFILE

HOSTS
New Zealand and Australia

WINNERS
New Zealand

WINNING CAPTAIN
David Kirk

MOST POINTS
126
Grant Fox (NZL)

MOST TRIES
6
Craig Green (NZL)
John Kirwan (NZL)

BIGGEST WINNING MARGIN
64
New Zealand 70-6 Italy

RESULTS SNAPSHOT

POOL A
Australia	19-6	England
Japan	18-21	USA
England	60-7	Japan
Australia	47-12	USA
England	34-6	USA
Australia	42-23	Japan

POOL B
Canada	37-4	Tonga
Ireland	6-13	Wales
Tonga	16-29	Wales
Canada	19-46	Ireland
Canada	9-40	Wales
Ireland	32-9	Tonga

POOL C
New Zealand	70-6	Italy
Argentina	9-28	Fiji
New Zealand	74-13	Fiji
Argentina	25-16	Italy
Fiji	15-18	Italy
New Zealand	46-15	Argentina

POOL D
Romania	21-20	Zimbabwe
France	20-20	Scotland
France	55-12	Romania
Scotland	60-21	Zimbabwe
Romania	28-55	Scotland
France	70-12	Zimbabwe

KNOCKOUT STAGE

QUARTER-FINALS

New Zealand **30-3** Scotland
Lancaster Park, Christchurch

Wales **16-3** England
Ballymore, Brisbane

France **31-16** Fiji
Eden Park, Auckland

Australia **33-15** Ireland
Concord Oval, Sydney

SEMI-FINALS

New Zealand **49-6** Wales
Ballymore, Brisbane

France **30-24** Australia
Concord Oval, Sydney

BRONZE FINAL

Wales **22-21** Australia
Rotorua International Stadium

THE FINAL
Eden Park, Auckland

NEW ZEALAND 29-9 FRANCE

Tries
Michael Jones, David Kirk
John Kirwan

Conversions
Grant Fox

Penalty Goals
Grant Fox (4)

Drop Goals
Grant Fox

Tries
Pierre Berbizier

Conversions
Didier Camberabero

Penalty Goals
Didier Camberabero

Attendance: 48,035 Referee: Kerry Fitzgerald (AUS)

RUGBY
WORLD CUP™
JAPAN 日本 2019

DON'T BE LET DOWN

ONLY BUY TICKETS FROM OFFICIAL SOURCES:

- REMAINING TICKETS ON GENERAL SALE NOW
- OFFICIAL HOSPITALITY PACKAGES STILL AVAILABLE
- TICKET-INCLUSIVE SUPPORTER TOUR PACKAGES AVAILABLE

FOR MORE INFORMATION VISIT
RUGBYWORLDCUP.COM/BUY-OFFICIAL

#RWC2019 [f] [y] [▶] [◉]

1991 TOURNAMENT STATS

POOL STAGE - FINAL STANDINGS

POOL A

Team	Wins	Draws	Losses	For	Against	Tries	Points
New Zealand	3	0	0	95	39	13	6
England	2	0	1	85	33	9	4
Italy	1	0	2	57	76	7	2
USA	0	0	3	24	113	2	0

*New Zealand and England advanced to the quarter-finals

POOL B

Team	Wins	Draws	Losses	For	Against	Tries	Points
Scotland	3	0	0	122	36	17	6
Ireland	2	0	1	102	51	12	4
Japan	1	0	2	77	87	13	2
Zimbabwe	0	0	3	31	158	6	0

*Scotland and Ireland advanced to the quarter-finals

POOL C

Team	Wins	Draws	Losses	For	Against	Tries	Points
Australia	3	0	0	79	25	11	6
W. Samoa	2	0	1	54	34	8	4
Wales	1	0	2	32	61	3	2
Argentina	0	0	3	38	83	4	0

*Australia and Western Samoa advanced to the quarter-finals

POOL D

Team	Wins	Draws	Losses	For	Against	Tries	Points
France	3	0	0	82	25	12	6
Canada	2	0	1	45	33	4	4
Romania	1	0	2	31	64	5	2
Fiji	0	0	3	27	63	1	0

*France and Canada advanced to the quarter-finals

FACTFILE

HOSTS
England, France, Ireland, Scotland, Wales

WINNERS
Australia

WINNING CAPTAIN
Nick Farr-Jones

MOST POINTS
68
Ralph Keyes (IRE)

MOST TRIES
6
Jean-Baptiste Lafond (FRA)
David Campese (AUS)

BIGGEST WINNING MARGIN
44
Ireland 55-11 Zimbabwe
Japan 52-8 Zimbabwe

RESULTS SNAPSHOT

England	**12-18**	New Zealand
Italy	**30-9**	USA
New Zealand	**46-6**	USA
England	**36-6**	Italy
England	**37-9**	USA
Italy	**21-31**	New Zealand

Scotland	**47-9**	Japan
Ireland	**55-11**	Zimbabwe
Ireland	**32-16**	Japan
Scotland	**51-12**	Zimbabwe
Scotland	**24-15**	Ireland
Japan	**52-8**	Zimbabwe

Australia	**32-19**	Argentina
W. Samoa	**16-13**	Wales
Australia	**9-3**	W. Samoa
Wales	**16-7**	Argentina
Australia	**38-3**	Wales
W. Samoa	**35-12**	Argentina

France	**30-3**	Romania
Canada	**13-3**	Fiji
France	**33-9**	Fiji
Canada	**19-11**	Romania
Romania	**17-15**	Fiji
France	**19-13**	Canada

KNOCKOUT STAGE

QUARTER-FINALS

Scotland	**28-6**	Western Samoa

Murrayfield, Edinburgh

England	**19-10**	France

Parc des Princes, Paris

Ireland	**18-19**	Australia

Lansdowne Road, Dublin

Canada	**13-29**	New Zealand

Lille-Metropole, Villeneuve d'Ascq

SEMI-FINALS

Scotland	**6-9**	England

Murrayfield, Edinburgh

Australia	**16-6**	New Zealand

Lansdowne Road, Dublin

BRONZE FINAL

New Zealand	**13-6**	Scotland

Cardiff Arms Park, Cardiff

THE FINAL

Twickenham Stadium, London

AUSTRALIA 12-6 ENGLAND

Tries:
Tony Daly

Conversions:
Michael Lynagh

Penalty Goals:
Michael Lynagh (2)

Penalty Goals:
Jon Webb (2)

Attendance: 56,000 **Referee:** Derek Bevan (WAL)

POOL STAGE - FINAL STANDINGS

POOL A

Team	Wins	Draws	Losses	For	Against	Tries	Points
South Africa	3	0	0	68	26	6	6
Australia	2	0	1	87	41	11	4
Canada	1	0	2	45	50	4	2
Romania	0	0	3	14	97	1	0

South Africa and Australia advanced to the quarter-finals

POOL B

Team	Wins	Draws	Losses	For	Against	Tries	Points
England	3	0	0	95	60	6	6
W. Samoa	2	0	1	96	88	12	4
Italy	1	0	2	69	94	7	2
Argentina	0	0	3	69	87	8	0

England and Western Samoa advanced to the quarter-finals

POOL C

Team	Wins	Draws	Losses	For	Against	Tries	Points
New Zealand	3	0	0	222	45	28	6
Ireland	2	0	1	93	94	13	4
Wales	1	0	2	89	68	9	2
Japan	0	0	3	55	252	8	0

New Zealand and Ireland advanced to the quarter-finals

POOL D

Team	Wins	Draws	Losses	For	Against	Tries	Points
France	3	0	0	114	47	13	6
Scotland	2	0	1	149	27	18	4
Tonga	1	0	2	44	90	6	2
Ivory Coast	0	0	3	29	172	3	0

France and Scotland advanced to the quarter-finals

FACTFILE

HOSTS
South Africa

WINNERS
South Africa

WINNING CAPTAIN
Francois Pienaar

MOST POINTS
112
Thierry Lacroix (FRA)

MOST TRIES
6
Jonah Lomu (NZL)
Marc Ellis (NZL)

BIGGEST WINNING MARGIN
128
New Zealand 145-17
Japan

RESULTS SNAPSHOT

POOL A

South Africa	**27-18**	Australia
Canada	**34-3**	Romania
South Africa	**21-8**	Romania
Australia	**27-11**	Canada
Australia	**42-3**	Romania
South Africa	**20-0**	Canada

POOL B

Italy	**18-42**	W. Samoa
Argentina	**18-24**	England
W. Samoa	**32-26**	Argentina
England	**27-20**	Italy
Argentina	**25-31**	Italy
England	**44-22**	W. Samoa

POOL C

Japan	**10-57**	Wales
Ireland	**19-43**	New Zealand
Ireland	**50-28**	Japan
New Zealand	**34-9**	Wales
Japan	**17-145**	New Zealand
Ireland	**24-23**	Wales

POOL D

Ivory Coast	**0-89**	Scotland
France	**38-10**	Tonga
France	**54-18**	Ivory Coast
Scotland	**41-5**	Tonga
Ivory Coast	**11-29**	Tonga
France	**22-19**	Scotland

KNOCKOUT STAGE

QUARTER-FINALS

France	**36-12**	Ireland

King's Park, Durban

South Africa	**42-14**	Western Samoa

Ellis Park, Johannesburg

England	**25-22**	Australia

Newlands, Cape Town

New Zealand	**48-30**	Scotland

Loftus Versfeld, Pretoria

SEMI-FINALS

South Africa	**19-15**	France

King's Park, Durban

New Zealand	**45-29**	England

Newlands, Cape Town

BRONZE FINAL

France	**19-9**	England

Loftus Versfeld, Pretoria

THE FINAL

Ellis Park, Johannesburg

SOUTH AFRICA 15-12 (AET) NEW ZEALAND

Penalty Goals:
Joel Stransky (3)

Drop Goals:
Joel Stransky (2)

Penalty Goals:
Andrew Mehrtens (3)

Drop Goals:
Andrew Mehrtens

Attendance: 62,000 **Referee:** Ed Morrison (ENG)

POOL STAGE - FINAL STANDINGS

POOL A

Team	Wins	Draws	Losses	For	Against	Tries	Points
South Africa	3	0	0	132	35	18	6
Scotland	2	0	1	120	58	15	4
Uruguay	1	0	2	42	97	4	2
Spain	0	0	3	18	122	0	0

South Africa advanced to the quarter-finals; Scotland advanced to quarter-final play-off

POOL B

Team	Wins	Draws	Losses	For	Against	Tries	Points
New Zealand	3	0	0	176	28	22	6
England	2	0	1	184	47	22	4
Tonga	1	0	2	47	171	4	2
Italy	0	0	3	35	196	2	0

New Zealand advanced to the quarter-finals; England advanced to quarter-final play-off

POOL C

Team	Wins	Draws	Losses	For	Against	Tries	Points
France	3	0	0	108	52	13	6
Fiji	2	0	1	124	68	14	4
Canada	1	0	2	114	82	12	2
Namibia	0	0	3	28	186	4	0

France advanced to the quarter-finals; Fiji advanced to quarter-final play-off

POOL D

Team	Wins	Draws	Losses	For	Against	Tries	Points
Wales	2	0	1	118	71	14	4
Argentina	2	0	1	83	51	3	4
Samoa	2	0	1	97	72	11	4
Japan	0	0	3	36	140	2	0

Wales advanced to the quarter-finals; Argentina and Samoa advanced to quarter-final play-off

POOL E

Team	Wins	Draws	Losses	For	Against	Tries	Points
Australia	3	0	0	135	31	19	6
Ireland	2	0	1	100	45	12	4
Romania	1	0	2	50	126	5	2
USA	0	0	3	52	135	5	0

Australia advanced to the quarter-finals; Ireland advanced to quarter-final play-off

FACTFILE

HOSTS
Wales

WINNERS
Australia

WINNING CAPTAIN
John Eales

MOST POINTS
102
Gonzalo Quesada
(ARG)

MOST TRIES
8
Jonah Lomu (NZL)

BIGGEST WINNING MARGIN
98
New Zealand 101-3
Italy

RESULTS SNAPSHOT

POOL A

Uruguay	27-15	Spain
South Africa	46-29	Scotland
Scotland	43-12	Uruguay
South Africa	47-3	Spain
South Africa	39-3	Uruguay
Scotland	48-0	Spain

POOL B

England	67-7	Italy
New Zealand	45-9	Tonga
New Zealand	30-16	England
Tonga	28-25	Italy
New Zealand	101-3	Italy
England	101-10	Tonga

POOL C

Fiji	67-18	Namibia
France	33-20	Canada
France	47-13	Namibia
Fiji	38-22	Canada
Canada	72-11	Namibia
France	28-19	Fiji

POOL D

Wales	23-18	Argentina
Samoa	43-9	Japan
Wales	64-15	Japan
Argentina	32-16	Samoa
Samoa	38-31	Wales
Argentina	33-12	Japan

POOL E

Ireland	53-8	USA
Australia	57-9	Romania
Romania	27-25	USA
Australia	23-3	Ireland
Australia	55-19	USA
Ireland	44-14	Romania

QUARTER-FINAL PLAY-OFFS

England	45-24	Fiji
Scotland	35-20	Samoa
Argentina	28-24	Ireland

KNOCKOUT STAGE

QUARTER-FINALS

Australia	**24-9**	Wales

Millennium Stadium, Cardiff

South Africa	**44-21**	England

Stade de France, Paris

New Zealand	**30-18**	Scotland

Murrayfield, Edinburgh

France	**47-26**	Argentina

Lansdowne Road, Dublin

SEMI-FINALS

Australia	**27-21**	South Africa

Twickenham, London

France	**43-31**	New Zealand

Twickenham, London

BRONZE FINAL

South Africa	**22-18**	New Zealand

Millennium Stadium, Cardiff

THE FINAL

Millennium Stadium, Cardiff

AUSTRALIA 35-12 FRANCE

Tries:
Owen Finegan, Ben Tune

Conversions:
Matthew Burke (2)

Penalty Goals:
Matthew Burke (7)

Penalty Goals:
Christophe Lamaison (4)

Attendance: 72,500 **Referee:** André Watson (RSA)

2003 TOURNAMENT STATS

POOL STAGE - FINAL STANDINGS

POOL A

Team	Wins	Draws	Losses	For	Against	Tries	Points
Australia	4	0	0	273	32	2	18
Ireland	3	0	1	141	56	3	15
Argentina	2	0	2	140	57	3	11
Romania	1	0	3	65	192	1	5
Namibia	0	0	4	28	310	0	0

*Australia and Ireland advanced to the quarter-finals

POOL B

Team	Wins	Draws	Losses	For	Against	Tries	Points
France	4	0	0	204	70	4	20
Scotland	3	0	1	102	97	2	14
Fiji	2	0	2	98	114	2	10
USA	1	0	3	86	125	2	6
Japan	0	0	4	79	163	0	0

*France and Scotland advanced to the quarter-finals

POOL C

Team	Wins	Draws	Losses	For	Against	Tries	Points
England	4	0	0	255	47	3	19
South Africa	3	0	1	184	60	3	15
Samoa	2	0	2	138	117	2	10
Uruguay	1	0	3	56	255	0	4
Georgia	0	0	4	46	200	0	0

*England and South Africa advanced to the quarter-finals

POOL D

Team	Wins	Draws	Losses	For	Against	Tries	Points
New Zealand	4	0	0	282	57	4	20
Wales	3	0	1	132	98	2	14
Italy	2	0	2	77	123	0	8
Canada	1	0	3	54	135	1	5
Tonga	0	0	4	46	178	1	1

*New Zealand and Wales advanced to the quarter-finals

FACTFILE

HOSTS
Australia

WINNERS
England

WINNING CAPTAIN
Martin Johnson

MOST POINTS
113
Jonny Wilkinson
(ENG)

MOST TRIES
8
Doug Howlett (NZL)
Mils Muliaina (NZL)

**BIGGEST WINNING
MARGIN**
142
Australia 142-0
Namibia

RESULTS SNAPSHOT

POOL A

Australia	**24-8**	Argentina
Ireland	**45-17**	Romania
Argentina	**67-14**	Namibia
Australia	**90-8**	Romania
Ireland	**64-7**	Namibia
Argentina	**50-3**	Romania
Australia	**142-0**	Namibia
Ireland	**16-15**	Argentina
Romania	**37-7**	Namibia
Australia	**17-16**	Ireland

POOL B

France	**61-18**	Fiji
Scotland	**32-11**	Japan
Fiji	**19-18**	USA
France	**51-29**	Japan
Scotland	**39-15**	USA
Fiji	**41-13**	Japan
France	**51-9**	Scotland
USA	**39-26**	Japan
France	**41-14**	USA
Scotland	**22-20**	Fiji

POOL C

South Africa	**72-6**	Uruguay
England	**84-6**	Georgia
Samoa	**60-13**	Uruguay
England	**25-6**	South Africa
Samoa	**46-9**	Georgia
South Africa	**46-19**	Georgia
England	**35-22**	Samoa
Uruguay	**24-12**	Georgia
South Africa	**60-10**	Samoa
England	**111-13**	Uruguay

POOL D

New Zealand	**70-7**	Italy
Wales	**41-10**	Canada
Italy	**36-12**	Tonga
New Zealand	**68-6**	Canada
Wales	**27-20**	Tonga
Italy	**19-14**	Canada
New Zealand	**91-7**	Tonga
Wales	**27-15**	Italy
Canada	**24-7**	Tonga
New Zealand	**53-37**	Wales

KNOCKOUT STAGE

QUARTER-FINALS

New Zealand **29-9** South Africa
Telstra Dome, Melbourne

Australia **33-16** Scotland
Suncorp Stadium, Brisbane

France **43-21** Ireland
Telstra Dome, Melbourne

England **28-17** Wales
Suncorp Stadium, Brisbane

SEMI-FINALS

Australia **22-10** New Zealand
Telstra Stadium, Sydney

England **24-7** France
Telstra Stadium, Sydney

BRONZE FINAL

New Zealand **40-13** France
Telstra Stadium, Sydney

THE FINAL
Telstra Stadium, Sydney

ENGLAND 20-17 AUSTRALIA
(AET)

Tries:
Jason Robinson

Penalty Goals:
Jonny Wilkinson (4)

Drop Goals:
Jonny Wilkinson

Tries:
Lote Tuqiri

Penalty Goals:
Elton Flatley (4)

Attendance: 82,957 **Referee:** André Watson (RSA)

We believe in the power of sport.
Nous croyons au pouvoir du sport.

Join World Rugby and ChildFund in changing lives for disadvantaged children in Asia so they can play, learn and grow.

Rejoignez World Rugby et ChildFund pour changer la vie des enfants défavorisés d'Asie pour qu'ils puissent jouer, apprendre et grandir.

POOL STAGE - FINAL STANDINGS

POOL A

Team	Wins	Draws	Losses	For	Against	Tries	Points
South Africa	4	0	0	189	47	3	19
England	3	0	1	108	88	2	14
Tonga	2	0	2	89	96	1	9
Samoa	1	0	3	69	143	1	5
USA	0	0	4	61	142	1	1

South Africa and England advanced to the quarter-finals

POOL B

Team	Wins	Draws	Losses	For	Against	Tries	Points
Australia	4	0	0	215	41	4	20
Fiji	3	0	1	114	136	3	15
Wales	2	0	2	168	105	4	12
Japan	0	1	3	64	210	1	3
Canada	0	1	3	51	120	0	2

Australia and Fiji advanced to the quarter-finals

POOL C

Team	Wins	Draws	Losses	For	Against	Tries	Points
New Zealand	4	0	0	309	35	4	20
Scotland	3	0	1	116	66	2	14
Italy	2	0	2	85	117	1	9
Romania	1	0	3	40	161	1	5
Portugal	0	0	4	38	209	1	1

New Zealand and Scotland advanced to the quarter-finals

POOL D

Team	Wins	Draws	Losses	For	Against	Tries	Points
Argentina	4	0	0	143	33	2	18
France	3	0	1	188	37	3	15
Ireland	2	0	2	64	82	1	9
Georgia	1	0	3	50	111	1	5
Namibia	0	0	4	30	212	0	0

Argentina and France advanced to the quarter-finals

FACTFILE

HOSTS
France

WINNERS
South Africa

WINNING CAPTAIN
John Smit

MOST POINTS
105
Percy Montgomery
(RSA)

MOST TRIES
8
Bryan Habana (RSA)

BIGGEST WINNING MARGIN
95
New Zealand 108-13
Portugal

RESULTS SNAPSHOT

POOL A

England	**28-10**	USA
South Africa	**59-7**	Samoa
Tonga	**25-15**	USA
South Africa	**36-0**	England
Tonga	**19-15**	Samoa
South Africa	**30-25**	Tonga
England	**44-22**	Samoa
Samoa	**25-21**	USA
England	**36-20**	Tonga
South Africa	**64-15**	USA

POOL B

Australia	**91-3**	Japan
Wales	**42-17**	Canada
Fiji	**35-31**	Japan
Australia	**32-20**	Wales
Fiji	**29-16**	Canada
Wales	**72-18**	Japan
Australia	**55-12**	Fiji
Canada	**12-12**	Japan
Australia	**37-6**	Canada
Fiji	**38-34**	Wales

POOL C

New Zealand	**76-14**	Italy
Scotland	**56-10**	Portugal
Italy	**24-18**	Romania
New Zealand	**108-13**	Portugal
Scotland	**42-0**	Romania
Italy	**31-5**	Portugal
New Zealand	**40-0**	Scotland
Romania	**14-10**	Portugal
New Zealand	**85-8**	Romania
Scotland	**18-16**	Italy

POOL D

Argentina	**17-12**	France
Ireland	**32-17**	Namibia
Argentina	**33-3**	Georgia
Ireland	**14-10**	Georgia
France	**87-10**	Namibia
France	**25-3**	Ireland
Argentina	**63-3**	Namibia
Georgia	**30-0**	Namibia
France	**64-7**	Georgia
Argentina	**30-15**	Ireland

KNOCKOUT STAGE

QUARTER-FINALS

England **12-10** Australia
Stade Velodrome, Marseille

France **20-18** New Zealand
Millennium Stadium, Cardiff

South Africa **37-20** Fiji
Stade Velodrome, Marseille

Argentina **19-13** Scotland
Stade de France, Paris

SEMI-FINALS

England **14-9** France
Stade de France, Paris

South Africa **37-13** Argentina
Stade de France, Paris

BRONZE FINAL

Argentina **34-10** France
Parc des Princes, Paris

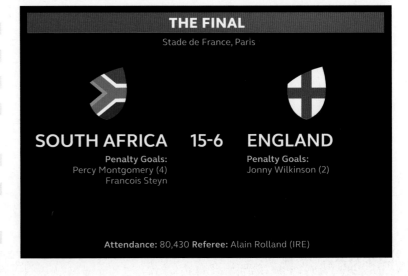

THE FINAL
Stade de France, Paris

SOUTH AFRICA 15-6 ENGLAND

Penalty Goals:
Percy Montgomery (4)
Francois Steyn

Penalty Goals:
Jonny Wilkinson (2)

Attendance: 80,430 Referee: Alain Rolland (IRE)

POOL STAGE - FINAL STANDINGS

POOL A

Team	Wins	Draws	Losses	For	Against	Tries	Points
New Zealand	4	0	0	240	49	4	20
France	2	0	2	124	96	3	11
Tonga	2	0	2	80	98	1	9
Canada	1	1	2	82	168	0	6
Japan	0	1	3	69	184	0	2

*New Zealand and France advanced to the quarter-finals

POOL B

Team	Wins	Draws	Losses	For	Against	Tries	Points
England	4	0	0	137	34	2	18
Argentina	3	0	1	90	40	2	14
Scotland	2	0	2	73	59	3	11
Georgia	1	0	3	48	90	0	4
Romania	0	0	4	44	169	0	0

*England and Argentina advanced to the quarter-finals

POOL C

Team	Wins	Draws	Losses	For	Against	Tries	Points
Ireland	4	0	0	135	34	1	17
Australia	3	0	1	173	48	3	15
Italy	2	0	2	92	95	2	10
USA	1	0	3	38	122	0	4
Russia	0	0	4	57	196	1	1

*Ireland and Australia advanced to the quarter-finals

POOL D

Team	Wins	Draws	Losses	For	Against	Tries	Points
South Africa	4	0	0	166	24	2	18
Wales	3	0	1	180	34	3	15
Samoa	2	0	2	91	49	2	10
Fiji	1	0	3	59	167	1	5
Namibia	0	0	4	44	266	0	0

*South Africa and Wales advanced to the quarter-finals

FACTFILE

HOSTS
New Zealand

WINNERS
New Zealand

WINNING CAPTAIN
Richie McCaw

MOST POINTS
62
Morné Steyn (RSA)

MOST TRIES
6
Chris Ashton (ENG)
Vincent Clerc (FRA)

BIGGEST WINNING MARGIN
87
South Africa 87-0 Namibia

RESULTS SNAPSHOT

POOL A

New Zealand	41–10	Tonga
France	47–21	Japan
Tonga	20–25	Canada
New Zealand	83–7	Japan
France	46–19	Canada
Tonga	31–18	Japan
New Zealand	37–17	France
Canada	23–23	Japan
France	14–19	Tonga
New Zealand	79–15	Canada

POOL B

Scotland	34-24	Romania
England	13-9	Argentina
Scotland	14-6	Georgia
Argentina	43-8	Romania
England	41-10	Georgia
England	67-3	Romania
Argentina	13-12	Scotland
Georgia	25-9	Romania
England	16-12	Scotland
Argentina	25-7	Georgia

POOL C

Australia	32–6	Italy
Ireland	22–10	USA
Russia	6–13	USA
Australia	6–15	Ireland
Italy	53–17	Russia
Australia	67–5	USA
Ireland	62–12	Russia
Italy	27–10	USA
Australia	68–22	Russia
Ireland	36–6	Italy

POOL D

Fiji	49–25	Namibia
South Africa	17–16	Wales
Samoa	49–12	Namibia
South Africa	49–3	Fiji
Wales	17–10	Samoa
South Africa	87–0	Namibia
Fiji	7–27	Samoa
Wales	81–7	Namibia
South Africa	13–5	Samoa
Wales	66–0	Fiji

KNOCKOUT STAGE

QUARTER-FINALS

Wales	22-10	Ireland

Regional Stadium, Wellington

France	19-12	England

Eden Park, Auckland

Australia	11-9	South Africa

Regional Stadium, Wellington

New Zealand	33-10	Argentina

Eden Park, Auckland

SEMI-FINALS

France	9-8	Wales

Eden Park, Auckland

New Zealand	20-6	Australia

Eden Park, Auckland

BRONZE FINAL

Australia	21-18	Wales

Eden Park, Auckland

THE FINAL

Eden Park, Auckland

NEW ZEALAND 8-7 FRANCE

Tries:
Tony Woodcock

Penalty Goals:
Stephen Donald

Tries:
Thierry Dusautoir

Conversions:
François Trinh-Duc

Attendance: 61,079 **Referee:** Craig Joubert (RSA)

2015 TOURNAMENT STATS

POOL STAGE - FINAL STANDINGS

POOL A

Team	Wins	Draws	Losses	For	Against	Tries	Points
Australia	4	0	0	141	35	17	17
Wales	3	0	1	111	62	11	13
England	2	0	2	133	75	16	11
Fiji	1	0	3	84	101	10	5
Uruguay	0	0	4	30	226	2	0

Australia and Wales advanced to the quarter-finals

POOL B

Team	Wins	Draws	Losses	For	Against	Tries	Points
South Africa	3	0	1	176	56	23	16
Scotland	3	0	1	136	93	14	14
Japan	3	0	1	98	100	9	12
Samoa	1	0	3	69	124	7	6
USA	0	0	4	50	156	5	0

South Africa and Scotland advanced to the quarter-finals

POOL C

Team	Wins	Draws	Losses	For	Against	Tries	Points
New Zealand	4	0	0	174	49	25	19
Argentina	3	0	1	179	70	22	15
Georgia	2	0	2	53	123	5	8
Tonga	1	0	3	70	130	8	6
Namibia	0	0	4	70	174	8	1

New Zealand and Argentina advanced to the quarter-finals

POOL D

Team	Wins	Draws	Losses	For	Against	Tries	Points
Ireland	4	0	0	134	35	16	18
France	3	0	1	120	63	12	14
Italy	2	0	2	74	88	7	10
Romania	1	0	3	60	129	7	4
Canada	0	0	4	58	131	7	2

Ireland and France advanced to the quarter-finals

FACTFILE

HOSTS
England

WINNERS
New Zealand

WINNING CAPTAIN
Richie McCaw

MOST POINTS
97
Nicolás Sánchez
(ARG)

MOST TRIES
8
Julian Savea (NZL)

BIGGEST WINNING MARGIN
64
South Africa 64-0 USA

RESULTS SNAPSHOT

POOL A

England	**35–11**	Fiji
Wales	**54–9**	Uruguay
Australia	**28–13**	Fiji
England	**25–28**	Wales
Australia	**65–3**	Uruguay
Wales	**23–13**	Fiji
England	**13–33**	Australia
Fiji	**47–15**	Uruguay
Australia	**15–6**	Wales
England	**60–3**	Uruguay

POOL B

South Africa	**32–34**	Japan
Samoa	**25–16**	USA
Scotland	**45–10**	Japan
South Africa	**46–6**	Samoa
Scotland	**39–16**	USA
Samoa	**5–26**	Japan
South Africa	**34–16**	Scotland
South Africa	**64–0**	USA
Samoa	**33–36**	Scotland
USA	**18–28**	Japan

POOL C

Tonga	**10–17**	Georgia
New Zealand	**26–16**	Argentina
New Zealand	**58–14**	Namibia
Argentina	**54–9**	Georgia
Tonga	**35–21**	Namibia
New Zealand	**43–10**	Georgia
Argentina	**45–16**	Tonga
Namibia	**16–17**	Georgia
New Zealand	**47–9**	Tonga
Argentina	**64–19**	Namibia

POOL D

Ireland	**50–7**	Canada
France	**32–10**	Italy
France	**38–11**	Romania
Italy	**23–18**	Canada
Ireland	**44–10**	Romania
France	**41–18**	Canada
Ireland	**16–9**	Italy
Canada	**15–17**	Romania
Italy	**32–22**	Romania
France	**9–24**	Ireland

KNOCKOUT STAGE

QUARTER-FINALS

South Africa	**23–19**	Wales

Twickenham Stadium, London

New Zealand	**62–13**	France

Millennium Stadium, Cardiff

Ireland	**20–43**	Argentina

Millennium Stadium, Cardiff

Australia	**35–34**	Scotland

Twickenham Stadium, London

SEMI-FINALS

South Africa	**18–20**	New Zealand

Twickenham Stadium, London

Argentina	**15–29**	Australia

Twickenham Stadium, London

BRONZE FINAL

South Africa	**24–13**	Argentina

Olympic Stadium, London

THE FINAL

Twickenham Stadium, London

NEW ZEALAND   34-17   AUSTRALIA

Tries: Nehe Milner-Skudder, Ma'a Nonu (1), Beauden Barrett

Conversions: Dan Carter (2)

Penalty Goals: Dan Carter (4)

Drop Goals: Dan Carter

Tries: David Pocock, Tevita Kuridrani

Conversions: Bernard Foley (2)

Penalty Goals: Bernard Foley

Attendance: 80,125 **Referee:** Nigel Owens (WAL)

POOL A

Fri 20 Sep - 19:45 - Tokyo Stadium
Japan v Russia

Sun 22 Sep - 16:45 - International Stadium Yokohama
Ireland v Scotland

Tues 24 Sep - 19:15 - Kumagaya Rugby Stadium
Russia v Samoa

Sat 28 Sep - 16:15 - Shizuoka Stadium Ecopa
Japan v Ireland

Mon 30 Sep - 19:15 - Kobe Misaki Stadium
Scotland v Samoa

Thurs 03 Oct - 19:15 - Kobe Misaki Stadium
Ireland v Russia

Sat 05 Oct - 19:30 - City of Toyota Stadium
Japan v Samoa

Wed 09 Oct - 16:15 - Shizuoka Stadium Ecopa
Scotland v Russia

Sat 12 Oct - 19:45 - Fukuoka Hakatanomori Stadium
Ireland v Samoa

Sun 13 Oct - 19:45 - International Stadium Yokohama
Japan v Scotland

POOL C

Sat 21 Sep - 16:15 - Tokyo Stadium
France v Argentina

Sun 22 Sep - 19:15 - Sapporo Dome
England v Tonga

Thurs 26 Sep - 19:45 - Kobe Misaki Stadium
England v USA

Sat 28 Sep - 13:45 - Hanazono Rugby Stadium
Argentina v Tonga

Wed 02 Oct - 16:45 - Fukuoka Hakatanomori Stadium
France v USA

Sat 05 Oct - 17:00 - Tokyo Stadium
England v Argentina

Sun 06 Oct - 16:45 - Kumamoto Stadium
France v Tonga

Wed 09 Oct - 13:45 - Kumagaya Rugby Stadium
Argentina v USA

Sat 12 Oct - 17:15 - International Stadium Yokohama
England v France

Sun 13 Oct - 14:45 - Hanazono Rugby Stadium
USA v Tonga

POOL B

Sat 21 Sep - 18:45 - International Stadium Yokohama
New Zealand v South Africa

Sun 22 Sep - 14:15 - Hanazono Rugby Stadium
Italy v Namibia

Thurs 26 Sep - 16:45 - Fukuoka Hakatanomori Stadium
Italy v Canada

Sat 28 Sep - 18:45 - City of Toyota Stadium
South Africa v Namibia

Wed 02 Oct - 19:15 - Oita Stadium
New Zealand v Canada

Fri 04 Oct - 18:45 - Shizuoka Stadium Ecopa
South Africa v Italy

Sun 06 Oct - 13:45 - Tokyo Stadium
New Zealand v Namibia

Tues 08 Oct - 19:15 - Kobe Misaki Stadium
South Africa v Canada

Sat 12 Oct - 13:45 - City of Toyota Stadium
New Zealand v Italy

Sun 13 Oct - 12:15 - Kamaishi Recovery Memorial Stadium
Namibia v Canada

POOL D

Sat 21 Sep - 13:45 - Sapporo Dome
Australia v Fiji

Mon 23 Sep - 19:15 - City of Toyota Stadium
Wales v Georgia

Wed 25 Sep - 14:15 - Kamaishi Recovery Memorial Stadium
Fiji v Uruguay

Sun 29 Sep - 14:15 - Kumagaya Rugby Stadium
Georgia v Uruguay

Sun 29 Sep - 16:45 - Tokyo Stadium
Australia v Wales

Thurs 03 Oct - 14:15 - Hanazono Rugby Stadium
Georgia v Fiji

Sat 05 Oct - 14:15 - Oita Stadium
Australia v Uruguay

Wed 09 Oct - 18:45 - Oita Stadium
Wales v Fiji

Fri 11 Oct - 19:15 - Shizuoka Stadium Ecopa
Australia v Georgia

Sun 13 Oct - 17:15 - Kumamoto Stadium
Wales v Uruguay

QF1

Sat 19 Oct - 16:15
Oita Stadium

WINNER POOL C

RUNNER-UP POOL D

QF2

Sat 19 Oct - 19:15
Tokyo Stadium

WINNER POOL B

RUNNER-UP POOL A

QF3

Sun 20 Oct - 16:15
Oita Stadium

WINNER POOL D

RUNNER-UP POOL C

QF4

Sun 20 Oct - 19:15
Tokyo Stadium

WINNER POOL A

RUNNER-UP POOL B

RUGBY
WORLD CUP
JAPAN 日本 2019

MATCH SCHEDULE

rugbyworldcup.com
#RWC2019

SEMI-FINALS

WINNER QF1	
WINNER QF2	

Sat 26 October   17:00 - International Stadium Yokohama

SEMI-FINALS

WINNER QF3	
WINNER QF4	

Sun 27 October   18:00 - International Stadium Yokohama

BRONZE FINAL

RUNNER-UP SF1	V	RUNNER-UP SF2

Fri 01 November   18:00 - Tokyo Stadium

FINAL

WINNER SF1	V	WINNER SF2

Sat 02 November   18:00 - International Stadium Yokohama

All matches are Japan Standard Time. Subject to change.

RUGBY
WORLD CUP™
JAPAN日本2019

Where did four years go?

It seems hard to believe now that Rugby World Cup 2015 happened so long ago.

That tournament had it all – thrills, packed stadiums, upsets, incredible action and fans from across the globe coming together in England and Cardiff to ensure a six-week rugby exhibition that showed off our sport in the best possible light.

At the time, 2019 seemed a distant point on the horizon and it felt like Japan had its work cut out to match the quality of the show put on at Twickenham and beyond.

Yet we need not have worried.

Since RWC 2015, the game has continued to grow and strengthen at the highest level and RWC 2019 looks set to be the most exciting and competitive Rugby World Cup of all time.

Everywhere you look there are sub-plots and unanswered questions aplenty.

Will Wales and Ireland lead the charge for the northern hemisphere? Can New Zealand make it three consecutive victories? Are Argentina again going to show their ongoing improvement by making their first final? Will Georgia underline again why the country is rugby crazy with another strong showing? Can Russia,

Canada or Namibia provide a stunning upset? Will England get back on track after such a poor showing at RWC 2015?

It is far too early – and difficult – to answer those questions and watching RWC 2019 unfurl and develop will make for fascinating viewing.

It is what happens off the pitch too that is sure to make RWC 2019 stand out as a truly remarkable tournament.

World Rugby deserve huge credit for reaching out to Asia in its ongoing bid to grow the sport and Japan has more than answered the call. There has never been pre-tournament excitement quite as pronounced and as prolific as that witnessed in Japan in recent months.

Volunteer numbers have been in their tens of thousands, ticket applications have been in the millions, seats are nearly all snapped up, every media outlet saturated with coverage, every day filled with excitement as the clock ticks down to what is sure to be the most popular tournament ever.

Japan will be the most amazing hosts imaginable, welcoming the world to its shores to show off the country – and rugby – in the best possible light.

Prepare to be amazed.